QUIET QUIT & FULLY LIVE

TAKE BACK YOUR TIME, ENERGY, AND LIFE THROUGH ETHICAL DISENGAGEMENT

MATTHEW HESS

Hylosis Publishing LLC
hylosis.pub

eBook ISBN-13: 979-8-89403-000-5

Paperback ISBN-13: 979-8-89403-001-2

Hardcover ISBN-13: 979-8-89403-002-9

To my wife Tessa, for your unwavering support and wisdom.

This book is a testament to the balance you bring to my life.

CONTENTS

FREE COMPANION WORKBOOK

As a thank you for spending your valuable time reading my book, I'm offering a free companion workbook to go along with it.

You can access it immediately here:

hylosis.pub/pages/free-content

It's a downloadable PDF that you can either fill in digitally, or print and write inside. Each chapter is distilled into key points, then there are prompts and exercises that follow the content of the book to help solidify the concepts in your own life. Examples include prompts for:

- **Exploring your motivations**

- **Determining your boundaries**

- **Building your Eisenhower Matrix**

- **Prioritizing the five different types of self-care**

If you want to fully leverage your time with the concepts laid out in this book, be sure to download the free companion workbook.

INTRODUCTION

IN THE RELENTLESS GRIND of the modern workplace, where "above and beyond" has become the expected norm, the pursuit of work-life balance has become an idealistic dream for many workers. While it is widely believed that perpetual overachievement is the only path to success, quiet quitting offers an alternative solution to reclaim control of your time, energy, and life. When done mindfully, saying "no" to extra work is not a career death sentence but rather a conscious choice to prioritize what truly matters.

Every worker has a unique story and faces unique challenges. For many, a point is reached when the demands of work spill too far into the enjoyment and fulfillment of life. Some employees find themselves stuck in a position that is mismatched with their skill sets or passions. Some realize that they're craving deeper social connections outside of work. Others feel called to travel the world or spend more time in nature. And some people experience such intense burnout that their vision is clouded and they are unsure exactly what they are seeking. Chances are, if you're reading this book, one or more of these scenarios may apply to you.

My own personal story hinged on changing life circumstances and a desire to be more present with my growing family. I was fortunate to have a job I enjoyed with people I liked, and I had always been happy to go "above and beyond" for my company. But once I became a father, I began to experience extreme guilt and sadness, realizing that my extended working times were robbing me of once-in-a-lifetime moments with my newborn firstborn son. I realized that the extra miles I'd been running were leading nowhere, and I knew it was time to change track.

At first, I had written off quiet quitting as an unethical option. But upon further research, I realized there were ethical ways I could apply the principles to benefit not only myself and my family, but also my employer. And believe it or not, it led to me becoming my boss's boss's boss (not a typo) with less stress, more pay, and—most importantly—more time.

Now, I'm eager to share everything I've learned about quiet quitting. In this book, I'll walk you through the myths I had to debunk and the mental blocks I had to overcome. I'll equip you with the strategies that helped me compartmentalize, manage my time, and set boundaries. And finally, I'll share the ways in which I was able to capitalize on the opportunities quiet quitting presented me—allowing me to ultimately feel like I was fully living.

It is important to note that not every aspect of quiet quitting will work for every job. Especially in regard to safety, you should never be cutting any corners. However, regardless of your position or situation, it is likely that some—if not all—of the strategies in this book can be adapted and applied.

The key is to think about how much you *can* handle versus how much you *should* handle. If you're working an entry-level job in retail or fast food but your boss is consistently asking you to take on management duties, you are likely being asked to handle more than you reasonably should. If you're in a project management role and additional tasks are consistently added to your plate at the last minute, it is likely that you're being expected to meet unrealistic expectations. Through strategic boundary setting and workflow optimization, you can realign with the requirements of your job while protecting your mental capacity.

As you walk through this book, the aim is that you'll come away with a better understanding of what quiet quitting actually means, what it doesn't mean, why people do it, and how to apply the parts of it that work for you.

1

WHAT IS QUIET QUITTING?

"[Today's] workers are demonstrating that they will not accept a lack of voice in the workplace, or employers who pay lip service to progressive values and then fall woefully short."
—Rebecca Givan, Professor of Labor Studies at Rutgers University

Quiet quitting versus slacking

QUIET QUITTING IS OFTEN perceived as fancy terminology for slacking on the job. Following this definition, quiet quitters can be seen as lazy and unwilling to put forth the effort required to do the jobs they are being paid to do.

With this in mind, it's understandable that quiet quitting is looked down upon by those who haven't taken the time to fully understand it. Articles can make the phenomenon sound particularly problematic. "Quiet quitting is destroying the workplace." "Quiet quitting is an invisible plague." One CNBC contributor even proclaimed that quiet quitting is "worse than COVID."[1]

In reality, these misconceptions stem from the expectations many employees are met with in today's workplace culture. An increasing number of employers have come to expect workers to perform far beyond their agreed-upon job duties. This leads to working environments where it is commonplace to say "yes" to every extra ask, setting aside any hope for work-life balance.

The concept of quiet quitting explores flipping this concept and prioritizing the employee's work-life balance. Rather than feeling pressured to accept every ask, successful quiet quitters learn to set and hold firm boundaries.

However, it is important to understand that successful quiet quitting should always include continuing to perform at least the minimum job duties required within the role, with all completed work done satisfactorily. Ideally, while the *amount* of work completed may change as a result of quiet quitting, the *quality* of the work should not change significantly. This is a notable distinction between slacking—when work quality will typically suffer—versus quiet quitting.

What about workers who are not taking on tasks beyond their agreed upon job duties but are still struggling with work-life balance—is quiet quitting an option for them? Likely, yes. These employees can benefit similarly from setting firm boundaries and implementing strategies to work more efficiently. We'll explore these concepts in chapters four, five, and six.

Addressing negative disengagement

Negative disengagement refers to feeling disinterested in all aspects of work. In some instances, negatively disengaged employees might hand in sloppily done work, not show up during work hours, or be unwilling to take on any task—even those clearly within their job descriptions. These types of behaviors directly conflict with quiet quitting, as the strategy relies on being able to continue performing essential job duties satisfactorily. If you choose to quiet quit, it will be important to stay vigilant to ensure you are continuously meeting the minimum requirements of your role.

Some factors leading employees to feel disengaged include:

- Low wages

- Inflexible work hours

- Losing ability to work from home

- Unclear job descriptions

- Lack of benefits

- Lack of opportunities for promotion

- Lack of constructive feedback[2]

Bottom line: our time is not inherently worth as much as it used to be to many employers in today's economy. It is up to us to change that.

How common is quiet quitting?

While some media outlets claim that quiet quitting is everywhere, the truth is that it is impossible to determine exactly how widespread it is.

A 2022 Gallup poll showed that 18% of Americans are "actively disengaged" from their work and almost 50% are simply "not engaged."[3] Taken together, this suggests that two-thirds of Americans are disengaged from their jobs. However, these statistics don't tell us how employees decide to move forward. While some may actively choose to quiet quit, others may fall into true slacking, and some may continue to push above and beyond despite disengagement.

It is further important to consider that when quiet quitting is done right, it can lead to increased job satisfaction and more engagement on the elements of work that matter most. Therefore, it is certainly possible that quiet quitters could be among the 32% of Americans who self-report as "actively engaged."

Since quiet quitting is "quiet" by definition, many employees implementing the strategy will not announce it by name. Therefore, the number of quiet quitters cannot easily be determined.

Is quiet quitting harmful to employers?

A common criticism of quiet quitting is that it is unfairly detrimental to employers.

Studies show that in the last year, as quiet quitting has gained popularity, employers as a whole have experienced lower overall productivity and growth.[4] However, despite media outlets using this as "proof" of the negative impact of quiet quitting, it is impossible to determine how much causation exists here. Other factors—such as the economy recovering from the pandemic and growing pains from remote working—could easily be impacting business success just as much, if not more.

Setting aside metrics and media portrayals, we can look objectively at the big picture of quiet quitting. If this strategy involves workers saying "no" to extra work that they previously would have taken on without hesitation, it makes sense that it could harm employer productivity to some degree. But is this the employee's responsibility?

The bottom line is that employees are responsible for performing their agreed-upon job duties. Employees are *not* responsible for taking on work outside of this scope, and therefore you should not feel guilty if you determine that you do not have the bandwidth to be able to do so. Career coach Allison Peck explains, "Choose carefully who you go above and beyond for and determine if it's worth it. Sometimes it pays off, but sometimes it doesn't."[5]

Secondly, consider that quietly quitting will do less harm to your employer than allowing yourself to become negatively disengaged. If you're experiencing poor working conditions or feeling yourself move toward burnout, quiet quitting may be able to help you stay afloat and continue performing your necessary job duties.

Lastly, it is important to note that quiet quitting can actually have a *positive* impact on employers as well. While this may seem counterintuitive, one of the top factors leading to high job satisfaction scores is good work-life balance.[6] Similarly, employees with the opportunity to tailor their work to their interests and abilities—something quiet quitting may give you more time and space to be able to do—report higher satisfaction.[7] Satisfied workers are likely to have a more positive net-impact within their jobs, and quiet quitting is one way to move toward higher satisfaction.

Should I be speaking up instead?

Some people considering quiet quitting hesitate in wondering whether they should be speaking up instead.

Proponents suggest "loudly persisting" may be a more effective strategy than quiet quitting. Loudly persisting refers to discussing your workplace issues with your boss, your company's senior management, your coworkers, and—in some cases—even the media.[8]

While loudly persisting can provide more opportunities to push for positive changes in your company or industry, there is no guarantee it will have this effect. Furthermore, loudly persisting will likely take even more time and energy than you are already expending on work.

Again, the determination on your best path forward—whether it's quiet quitting, loudly persisting, or continuing as-is—will be highly dependent on your specific situation and reasoning. If you are experiencing specific injustices in your workplace that you want to ensure do not continue, loudly persisting may be beneficial. However, if you're looking to realign priorities to focus more of your time and energy outside of work, quiet quitting will likely help.

Most importantly, consider that quiet quitting and loudly persisting do not have to be mutually exclusive. For example, you could opt to quiet quit while still loudly persisting about a specific element of your work. Additionally, any decision you make can be reassessed and adjusted at any time. Perhaps it makes sense to quiet quit while you're in a certain phase of life, giving yourself increased energy to come back and loudly persist in the future. Maintaining a flexible mindset and keeping your goals in mind will be key in finding the strategies that work best for you.

The importance of work-life balance

Work-life balance refers to the amount of time you spend doing your job compared with the amount of time you spend with your family and doing things you enjoy.[9] Quiet quitting, in a nutshell, is a way to build a work-life balance that better fits your unique situation.

Achieving optimal work-life balance means finding ways to split your time and energy effectively, enabling you to feel fulfilled both inside and outside of work. Benefits may include:

- Improved mental health

- Increased time to pursue activities you enjoy

- Expanded space to think and act creatively

- More focus to spend on family and friends

While finding work-life balance can sometimes be viewed as a selfish endeavor that only benefits an employee personally, it is shown to improve the work quality of employees as well. Optimal brain function, which is essential for good work, relies on physical and mental well-being.[10] Intentionally stepping away from work also gives you a chance to gain a new perspective, often helping to solve problems in more innovative ways. Chapter two will further explore the psychology behind burnout and how allowing your brain to relax and recharge will lead to better work in the long-term.

It is important to note that while the concept of work-life balance is fairly straightforward, the specifics can look very different from person to person. It may be difficult to find work-life balance if you are unsure which aspects of work and life are most important to you. Chapter three will help you determine these factors.

Finding new opportunities through quiet quitting

Another distinct benefit of quiet quitting is having the time and energy to explore new possibilities.

Maggie Perkins, a 30-year-old mother of three, is an example of this. She decided to quiet quit her teaching job in 2018, stating, "There was no reason for me to hustle because as a teacher, there are no promotion opportunities." Maggie defines quiet quitting as "doing your job only during contract hours—not taking on extra work—because that's how you get burned out or taken advantage of."[11]

Not only was Maggie feeling overworked and overwhelmed, but her daughter's daycare was charging her $1 per minute for late pickup each day. This wasn't sustainable, so she turned to quiet quitting out of necessity. However, soon after, she found a new world of possibility she'd never dreamed of. With newfound time and energy, Maggie was able to reconsider what type of work she wanted to be doing. Ultimately, she made the decision to leave teaching and became an academic consultant and tutor. In an interview with CNBC, Maggie explained that she is now willing to go above and beyond because she has found a healthy work environment at a company that truly values her.[12]

When you're focused solely on work, it can be hard to see the myriad of possibilities available to you. Quiet quitting not only gives you the space to see new possibilities, but also allows for the ability to act on pursuing different avenues you feel passionate about. Whether it's finding a new professional path, strengthening existing relationships, or finding a new hobby, quiet quitting can give you the freedom to broaden your trajectory.

Assessing the potential drawbacks of quiet quitting

With any decision, it's important to consider both the pros and cons. The bulk of this chapter has discussed the positive effects of quiet quitting, but it would be irresponsible not to address the potential negative outcomes as well.

While we've already debunked the idea that quiet quitting equals poor performance, understand that this will take some upfront strategic planning to be executed successfully. If you decide to quiet quit on a whim—without making a plan—it is likely that the quality of your work will suffer. Of course, this could lead to a slew of issues including workplace conflict, ineligibility for promotions, or even termination from your job.

This is why the key to successful quiet quitting is in finding ways to be more strategic with your time. Many quiet quitters state that their employers did not notice a difference, as they were able to complete all their required work more efficiently.[13]

But if you are currently taking on large amounts of extra work, dropping the extra tasks is sure to draw negative attention from your employer, right? Not necessarily. I mentioned in the introduction of this book that quiet quitting had the opposite impact for me. While training myself to re-prioritize my work, I gained a keen focus on which parts of it were essential to my company. As I found ways to optimize efficiency and save time on repetitive tasks, I was able to share best practices with my bosses and teammates. Indirectly, quiet quitting pushed me into behaviors that made me a more valuable employee, which led to quicker promotions than I thought were possible.

So how do you avoid the pitfalls of negative work performance and reap the benefits quiet quitting can have? Chapters four, five, and six will arm you with a variety of strategies to enforce boundaries, prioritize tasks, and effectively manage your workload.

Recapping chapter one

In this chapter, we addressed common misconceptions about quiet quitting and uncovered truths about how the positive impact it can bring to both workers and employers. Key takeaways include:

- Quiet quitting revolves around prioritizing work-life balance, requiring you to set and hold firm boundaries.

- When quiet quitting is done right, it should not result in negative work performance. A key element of quiet quitting is continuing to complete the minimum requirements of your job.

- Creating optimal work-life balance not only leads to improved mental health and increased time for your personal priorities, but is also likely to improve your quality of work by allowing your brain to function more effectively and exposing you to new perspectives.

- Quiet quitting is not "one size fits all"—it will need to be adapted to fit your personal situation. To increase your chance of success, it is important to consider your "why" and to set realistic goals.

- Whatever decision you make does not need to be permanent; you can (and should) continue to reassess and adjust your strategy often.

- Quiet quitting can give you space to fully explore new possibilities.

- The key to successful quiet quitting is in finding ways to be more strategic with your time.

For many, avoiding or reversing burnout is a major motivator in their decision to quiet quit. Now that you have an understanding of what quiet quitting is (and what it isn't), we'll dive into learning how you can use it to reverse the long-term impacts of stress.

2

UNDERSTANDING THE IMPACT OF STRESS AND BURNOUT

"The straw that breaks the camel's back always looks light enough, until it lands."
—Edgar Cantero, writer and cartoonist

Why is it important to understand stress?

IMAGINE THIS: ONE DAY at work, as you're about to leave for lunch, your boss stops you to ask that you send out a few more emails by the end of the day. It's not a lot of work—or particularly challenging—by itself, but the thought of adding those emails to your to-do list gives you an immediate headache. Suddenly, the amount of work that lies ahead of you feels insurmountable. You feel exhausted and overwhelmed knowing that this isn't just a one-time ask, but a pattern repeating itself again and again.

If you've experienced a scenario leading you to feel this way at work, you're certainly not alone. Two-thirds of Americans report feeling highly stressed, overwhelmed, or out of control at work.[14] Most report that this is due to an insurmountable workload that they feel they can never keep up with.

Not only does stress take its toll physically—often through headaches and loss of sleep—but it also makes you work less efficiently. One third of Americans lose up to an hour of working time every day due to stress.[15] In short, the more stressed you are, the harder it becomes to do your work; it's a self-perpetuating cycle. Worse, the more stressed you are, the more a single additional piece of work will increase your overall stress level.

Why is this cycle so problematic? And more importantly, how can you escape it? This chapter explores the psychology of stress and burnout and highlights how quiet quitting can help you rewire your brain to make stressors feel less stressful.

Your brain on stress

Stress is similar to narcotic use in the way it lights up some parts of your brain while withering others. Feeling stressed—especially for long periods of time—can have a measurably negative impact on you and your brain.

Picture your brain as a rubber band. When you experience stress, the rubber band stretches. Once the stress passes, the band returns to its original shape. This ability to adapt to changing circumstances and continue to function is called neuroplasticity, and it's what enables humans to learn such a wide variety of skills—from playing the piano to baking a perfect croissant. Neuroplasticity is also to credit for humans being able to thrive in less-than-ideal circumstances.[16] This brain flexibility is one of humanity's biggest advantages.

However, there's a limit to this flexibility—if you continue stretching a rubber band over and over, it will eventually become looser and will not return to the same shape. Similar results come from keeping a rubber band fully stretched for days or weeks on end. This is your brain rewiring itself in response to repeated or constant stress.

When learning a new skill, this rewiring process is highly beneficial. When practicing playing the same song on the piano each day, you'll learn to play it from memory. When perfecting your croissant recipe, you'll gain a keen sense for small improvements that can be made with each bake. But when it comes to stress, this process can perpetuate issues. If you experience stressful situations every day at work, you may start to feel stressed before you even start your shift. In this way, neuroplasticity can work against you by reinforcing patterns of stress and anxiety.[17]

Within your brain, three main stress-induced changes are happening: dendritic shrinkage, stress associations, and myelin overproduction.

Dendritic shrinkage

Dendritic shrinkage is the process in which the "arms"—known as dendrites—of your neurons reduce in size. Your neurons use their dendrites to communicate with other neurons and pass signals through the brain and the rest of your nervous system, allowing you to think, move, and respond to stimuli. Reduction in the size of dendrites means that this communication between neurons happens more slowly, in a different way, or—in extreme cases—not at all. In the short term, you may feel foggy, confused, and less able to focus.

In the long-term, dendritic shrinkage can be the first step toward a variety of neurodegenerative diseases.[18] People who are stressed over long periods of time can have a higher likelihood of developing neurological conditions such as anxiety, sleep loss, and even Alzheimer's and other memory issues.[19]

Stress associations

Stress associations have a negative influence on your thought patterns, though primarily short-term. The more you experience a certain stimulus followed by another, the more you'll link those two stimuli in your brain. Associations are happening when dogs begin to drool upon hearing a bell because their dinner always comes afterwards, or when mice panic at the sound of a tone which is always followed by a shock.[20]

Similarly, if you regularly find yourself stressed at work, you might start to notice yourself feeling stressed as you start your commute or even when simply thinking about work. This rewiring of your brain means that even if there's nothing particularly stressful happening at work on a specific day, you'll still have a stress reaction and the negative impact that comes with it.

Myelin overproduction

Myelin is a type of insulation that forms on neurons you often use together, allowing you to complete similar processes more quickly in the future. This helps with learning dance choreography, typing quickly, or—unfortunately—feeling your heartbeat increase as soon as you see a concerning email.

During stressful situations, myelin often forms on neurons in the white matter of your brain, where communication between regions takes p lace.[21] This is helpful in life-or-death situations when you see a stimulus and need to react quickly, but not as helpful in most workplace scenarios, as it limits your ability to problem solve effectively. This is why you may find yourself struggling to make good decisions in times of particular stress—and, over time, these changes in myelination can become long-lasting or even permanent.[22]

The effects

While you are not likely to notice the specific changes happening inside of your brain, you may experience any or all of the following stress symptoms:

- Sleep problems

- Negative mood

- Avoidance of stressful stimuli

- Intrusive thoughts of stressful situations

- Feeling dazed or like you are drifting through your day

- Upset stomach

- Headaches

- Chest pain

Burnout

Each person's brain has a capacity for the mental load it can handle.[23] The specific capacity varies by person and changes over time. As capacity is exceeded, stress turns to burnout. At this point, even small, easily achievable tasks may feel overwhelming or impossible.

As a brain continues to operate under stress over a long period of time, mental capacity is reduced and responding to new challenges becomes more difficult. Over a lifetime, this can lead to becoming more reactive and responding quickly with anger or frustration.[24] As you can likely imagine, these changes work together to make you more irritable, less able to remember things, worse at problem solving, and generally more stressed, more often.

Using plasticity to our advantage

While the long-term impacts of stress may feel concerning, the good news is that we can also use our brains' plasticity to our advantage. Now that you're aware of how stress can turn into a self-perpetuating cycle, we can explore how to reverse the effects.

As you may have guessed, the key to reducing the negative impacts of stress is to undo the processes causing the stress. Stress reinforces certain pathways in your brain and cuts off others, making white matter more active than grey matter and smothering your brain in stress hormones. When you are *not* stressed, the opposite happens—positive associations are reinforced, gray matter is built, and your nervous system is better able to handle new challenges.[25]

So how can you go about actively reducing your levels of stress? Here are a few suggestions you can consider implementing immediately:

- **Write down your to-do list.** This frees up mental capacity to think about other things, as you won't need to focus on remembering what to work on next.

- **Practice mindfulness.** While telling yourself to "relax" often has the opposite effect, finding a tangible activity that *helps* you to mindfully relax can be incredibly beneficial. You may consider mindful breathing, meditation, or taking a warm bath—any activity that feels relaxing to you can work.

- **Get some movement.** This actively combats stress by reducing stress hormones and releasing endorphins. Feel free to get creative—you don't have to go to the gym unless you want to. Taking a walk or spontaneously dancing around your living room will give you similar benefits.

- **Positively redirect your thoughts.** When you notice negative thoughts or fears creeping in, actively challenge them. Remind yourself of situations you've made it through in the past and consider your strengths. This conscious redirection reinforces new neural pathways in your brain, helping to reframe problems as challenges you look forward to over coming.[26]

These simple strategies can go a long way toward reducing stress in the moment, but they don't take anything off of your plate. If you're still finding yourself feeling overwhelmed by work, this is where quiet quitting comes in. Pairing the ability to stay mindful of stress levels with finding ways to create an optimal work-life balance can have a massive impact, pushing you toward a healthier and more relaxed life.

Recapping chapter two

While much of this chapter dives into the science of brain chemistry, these are a few of the distilled takeaways:

- Stress takes a toll both physically and mentally, and impacts your ability to work effectively.

- Burnout can cause even the smallest tasks to feel impossible.

- The more stress your brain experiences, the more your mental capacity for stress reduces, making it more difficult to "bounce back."

- Over time, stress can lead to difficulty problem solving, irritability, and—in extreme cases—even neurodegenerative diseases.

- Thankfully, the same brain function that can perpetuate stress can also work in our favor, meaning that we can re-train our brains to work through stress more effectively.

- Actively challenging yourself to think positively can go a long way toward reversing stress.

The next chapter will explore how to determine your "why" and set your goals as you consider whether quiet quitting is a path you want to pursue.

3

FINDING YOUR WHY AND SETTING YOUR GOALS

"Time is really the only capital that any human being has, and the only thing he can't afford to lose."

—Thomas Edison, inventor

Assessing your aspirations

NOW THAT WE'VE UNCOVERED the many benefits of improving work-life balance and reducing stress, it's time to deep-dive into your personal motivators.

If you found yourself with two extra hours in every day, how would you want to spend them? Would spending more quality time with loved ones be your top priority? Would you choose to take more leisurely walks with your dog? Do you have a passion project—or maybe an idea for one you never got to start—that you're dying to work on? Do you simply want more sleep?

Finding motivations that resonate with you will help to set you up for success, ensuring that quiet quitting effectively moves you toward living the full life you desire. In this chapter, we'll take a look at some of the most common scenarios faced by quiet quitters. You may find that one of these matches your situation exactly, but more likely, you'll see pieces of your situation in multiple different scenarios.

Note that while this chapter talks broadly about motivations, getting specific and intentional about your own is important. As you read, start thinking about your personal motivations and the goals you'd like to achieve through quiet quitting.

More time for passions and relationships

For many quiet quitters, the desire to spend more time on their passions is a major factor in their decision. From traveling the world to learning to knit or running around the yard with kids—passions come in all forms and are deeply personal.

Dr. Maria Kordowicz, an associate professor in organizational behavior, explains that a primary motivation for quiet quitting is, "people protecting time to reconnect with nature, travel and spend time with one another, helping to uphold their spiritual and psychological beliefs."[27] In short, many people quiet quit to prioritize their mental health in the form of finding more time for the activities that bring them joy.

During the workday, if you constantly find yourself daydreaming about being in your garden or simply unwinding by playing your favorite game, you are likely motivated—at least in part—by the desire to dedicate additional time to your passions. There may be one very specific passion you have in mind that you'd like to dedicate all of your extra time to, or your heart may be pulling you in several different directions. Either way, quiet quitting can provide you with increased flexibility to spend more of your time and mental resources on the things that are most important to you.

Generally, this shift to focus more energy on personal passions comes with a slew of positive effects. People who pursue hobbies report being more creative, gaining new perspectives, and even increasing their confidence.[28] Creative hobbies particularly improve performance and help better develop problem-solving skills.[29] Beyond that, spending time doing things you're passionate about boosts your mental health and motivation by improving your mood.

Seeking out new opportunities

If you've found yourself wanting something more out of life—even if you're not sure what—quiet quitting can provide space for you to explore a variety of avenues to find new passions you may have never thought of before.

Maybe you've come to the realization that you're in a toxic work environment, or perhaps opportunity for the professional growth you seek has stalled in your current role. Quiet quitting can give you more time to search for a new job or side venture that better aligns with your values and goals. You may even discover that you'd like to pursue a completely different path. The story of Maggie Perkins, discussed in chapter one, highlights that quiet quitting can allow you to step back, analyze your path, and carefully consider alternatives.

Or maybe you're generally happy with your job—or at least, you would be happy there if you weren't overworking yourself—but you want to find new passions outside of work. Quiet quitting can provide you with time to learn a new language, train for a marathon, or pursue dating in search of your ideal life partner. The possibilities are virtually endless.

Reversing burnout and improving mental health

Maybe you're feeling so burnt out that you simply cannot keep up your current level of work any longer. This reason for quiet quitting is equally valid and completely understandable. In chapter two, we learned that extreme stress and burnout can impact your ability to problem solve and react rationally. By quiet quitting, you can allow your brain the time it needs to reverse the perpetuating cycle of stress. Eventually, once you've taken the time to recover, you can slowly start exploring more ways to fill your newfound "free time."

Symptoms that could indicate that you're experiencing burnout include:

- Becoming cynical or critical at work

- Tiredness or apathy

- Irritability and impatience

- Lack of energy

- Difficulty concentrating

- Lack of satisfaction with work

- Changing sleep patterns

- Use of food, alcohol, or drugs as coping or numbing strategies

- Unexplained headaches or stomach problems[30]

People suffering from workplace stress will often report wishing that time would just stand still for a little while so they could catch up or will joke that they need a vacation desperately.[31] If you've started to realize that you aren't joking anymore, it could be a sign that your stress levels are too high.

However, prior to making the decision to quiet quit, it is important to consider whether work-related stressors are truly the source of your burnout. Step back to analyze what else is going on in your life—are there any family troubles or relationship struggles contributing to your mental load? If the answer is yes, this doesn't necessarily mean that quiet quitting will not be helpful, but it does mean that it likely will not fix all of your problems. Instead, in these situations, the biggest benefit of

quiet quitting may be gaining additional time to work through your othe
r difficulties.

Depending on the specifics and the severity of your situation, it could
also be beneficial to consider speaking with a therapist or counselor. If
this feels out of reach, below are a few additional options.

- Look into any potential employee assistant program (EAP)
  benefits through your work, school, or private insur-
  ance—these often include free or reduced access to therapy or
  counseling.

- Consider online therapy, such as BetterHelp or Talkspace.
  These options are typically more accessible and lower cost versus in-person therapy.[32]

- Try a free program, such as the interactive therapy program
  through Centre for Interactive Mental Health Solutions or the
  24/7 chat through 7 Cups.

- In an emergency, call or text 998 for assistance through the
  National Suicide Prevention Lifeline.

Summing up your goals

Most commonly, motivations for quiet quitting include a mix of the
scenarios covered in this chapter. You may simultaneously feel burnt out
from overworking, want to spend more time with your family, and wish
to engage in self-exploration.

To dive deeper into your unique situation, use the following questions
to gain further insight into your goals:

- Why do you want to make a change to your current work
  patterns?

- What do you hope to gain through quiet quitting?

- How do you foresee your *work life* looking in the weeks following your decision to quiet quit?

- How do you foresee your *life outside of work* looking in the weeks following your decision to quiet quit?

- Are there other strategies you should consider implementing in tandem with quiet quitting?

If you don't know the answers to all of these questions yet, that's okay. You can take note of your current answers and continue to refine them as you walk through the rest of this book. If you feel comfortable, discussing your responses with a trusted friend, family member, or counselor can also be helpful in challenging your initial reactions and encouraging you to dive deeper.

Recapping chapter three

This chapter explored a few different paths that commonly lead people to consider quiet quitting. Key takeaways are included below.

- Asking yourself how you'd ideally like to spend extra time in a day is a simple way to point you toward your "why."

- One of the most common reasons people quiet quit is to dedicate more time to passions outside of work—family, friends, hobbies, travel, and more!

- Quiet quitting can also give you the time to discover *new* passions and opportunities—including new paths for work, if desired.

- While quiet quitting can greatly reduce stress, it's important to determine the sources of your stress prior to implementing the strategy so you can set realistic expectations about how it will help.

- Your scenario is unique to you, so it is important for you to assess your goals prior to quiet quitting. You can continue to adjust these as you go.

In the next chapter, we'll start diving into ways to set and enforce internal boundaries—the heart of the quiet quitting strategy.

4

DETERMINING YOUR LIMITS AND ENFORCING INTERNAL BOUNDARIES

"If you want to live an authentic, meaningful life, you need to master the art of disappointing and upsetting others, hurting feelings, and living with the reality that some people just won't like you. It may not be easy, but it's essential if you want your life to reflect your deepest desires, values, and needs."

—Cheryl Richardson, author

The importance of boundaries

LEARNING TO SET AND enforce boundaries is the core importance of quiet quitting, as this enables you to define your work on your terms. In this process, focus is shifted to prioritize respect for your time and energy over other people's expectations—opening up the possibility for you to fully live.

For some people, the word "boundaries" may bring up strong associations, either positive or negative. Before fully diving into this chapter, take a moment to consider your preconceived notions of boundaries and challenge whether they align with your current goals.

The definition of boundaries is simple—it refers to placing limits on what you are willing to do. When considered carefully and implemented effectively, they can have a positive impact not only on your own mental health, but on your relationships with coworkers and the quality of your work as well. In today's interconnected world, it is easier than ever for lines between personal life and professional life to blur. While this is not always inherently a problem, it can become one when boundaries are not considered ahead of time and stuck to.

When making the decision to quiet quit and fully live, boundaries will need to be one of your most important considerations. These boundaries will hold the space you need to make room for all areas of your life to thrive. While boundary-setting can feel challenging—perhaps even overwhelming—at first, it brings a multitude of long-term benefits:

- **Stress reduction** is a major benefit of setting and enforcing boundaries. When boundaries are set effectively, you should (at least eventually) find yourself with more manageable amounts of work and more reasonable standards.

- **Increased productivity** may not seem as obviously related to setting boundaries, but it is often another result. Boundary-setting can help you align yourself with tasks that better match your interests and skill sets, and it will allow you to better prioritize tasks in the ways that work most effectively for you.

- **Strengthened mutual respect** between you, your colleagues, your clients, and/or your boss is also likely to result from clear communication of boundaries. People you work with will better understand how to support you, and they may even feel more comfortable sharing their own boundaries as well.

- **Reduced conflict** is another likely long-term benefit—chapter five will explore ways to clearly communicate limits early, leading to less chance of push-back or disappointment when you enforce a boundary.

- **Improved mental health** is likely to come alongside these benefits. Enforcing boundaries helps protect you against work-related burnout, anxiety, and depression.

While your boundaries will be specific to you, this chapter will provide you with general guidelines for defining, implementing, and enforcing them.

Defining your boundaries

Boundaries can generally be categorized in four ways: mental, physical, personal, and procedural.[33] As you read through the following examples, begin to think about which types of boundaries make the most sense for your unique situation.

Mental boundaries exist for you to protect your opinions, values, and beliefs. They can include:

- Giving yourself permission not to do things perfectly

- Defining which tasks you want to do and which you are okay with setting aside

- Making the decision not to check work email outside of working hours

- Choosing not to engage in workplace gossip or other challenging conversations

Physical boundaries relate to your physical presence in your work environment. These can include:

- Closing your office door or going to a quiet working space at certain times of the day

- Utilizing a workspace that is separate from your living space

Personal boundaries address how you'll interact with others. Examples include:

- Saying "no" to unreasonable requests

- Asking for help when needed

- Defining times when you are okay with being interrupted and times when you need to focus

- Limiting contact with people if needed

Finally, **procedural** boundaries define how you'll go about completing your tasks and moving throughout your workday. These can include:

- Defining the number of edits you'll do on a piece of work

- Requesting specifics for a project in writing

- Setting deadlines for incoming requests so that you have ample time to review them

- Creating a routine to complete before and after work to help you mentally shift in and out of "work mode"

A few considerations you may want to think about when setting your boundaries include:

- How many hours are you willing to work per day or per week? Are there specific restrictions you'll have on certain days?

- How much are you willing to help your colleagues?

- What are you absolutely not willing to do? (i.e. take on new tasks with little notice, stay late on Friday evenings, attend unnecessary meetings that are longer than half an hour)

Lastly, consider how firm your boundaries can and should reasonably be. This may vary by boundary, but considering this ahead of time can help you avoid the trap of "just this once" snowballing into your boundaries falling apart completely. Consciously building flexibility into your boundaries can help increase the chances that you'll be able to stick with them. For example, if you've created a boundary about not staying late on Fridays but you know there are occasional important meetings that come up during this time, perhaps you modify the boundary to state that you are willing to stay no more than one hour late, you must know at least one day in advance, and you will not make this exception more than once a month.

The more thought you put into specifying your boundaries and exceptions, the easier it will be to hold them.

Enforcing your boundaries

Often times, the most challenging part of sticking to boundaries doesn't involve anyone else—it involves resistance within your own mind.

Especially if you are used to over-performing in your role, it may be tempting to let your boundaries slide "just once" when you're the only one who will know about it. Maybe you want to answer one important email after working hours or attend just one extra meeting.

When these situations arise, it's important to consider why you feel the need to push your boundaries. Is the exception truly important, or are you simply falling back into old patterns because that's what feels most comfortable?

If you determine that the exception is worth it, it's not necessarily a bad thing to go against the boundaries you've set. However, you should use this to reconsider the parameters of the boundary. Can you further clarify when you're okay with making exceptions? Putting these examples in writing will help to ensure that "just this once" doesn't turn into an everyday occurrence.

On the other hand, if you determine that an exception is *not* worth making, you may want to explore additional ways to enforce your boundaries with yourself. If you can't stop yourself from checking your work email while you're spending time with family, perhaps you consider setting limits on your phone that prevent you from opening certain applications at certain times. If your job allows, you may even consider removing work applications and accounts from your personal devices altogether.

Some boundaries may require more creative solutions for enforcement. If you want to make sure you leave work on time every day, maybe you set an alarm thirty minutes beforehand to help shift yourself into wrap-up mode. If you want to reduce your time spent going through work emails each morning, you may choose to use a timer to keep yourself on track. Keep in mind that while these solutions are tools to help you stick to your boundaries, you're still going to have to do the work to enforce them.

Mental boundaries are often some of the hardest to enforce—particularly when trying to force yourself not to think about work. For these cases, purposeful distractions can be especially helpful. As soon as you notice yourself ruminating on something that isn't beneficial, try pushing yourself to do something else. You may find it beneficial to make two lists—one of relaxing or fun activities that bring you joy, such as reading or taking a bath, and a second of personal (not work-related) to-do items, such as cleaning around the house or meal prepping. Whenever you're not sure how to fill your time, you can reference these lists to choose an activity that will bring you benefit in one way or another.

Lastly, give yourself grace when you do slip up and go against the intentions of your boundaries. Rather than beating yourself up, consider the circumstances and brainstorm whether there are any ways to minimize the chances of this happening regularly. If you find yourself majorly stressing on Sunday about a presentation on Monday, perhaps you can plan for additional prep time next Friday. Or, you may find that it's easier to focus on productive tasks on Saturdays while filling Sunday afternoons with more fun and engaging activities.

As discussed in chapter two, thought processes and actions you repeat will become reinforced in your brain. If you believe that your boundaries are worthwhile, continue pushing to enforce them. Over time, it will become easier and more natural to shift your focus to more productive or positive thoughts and activities.

Where to start

Depending on your situation, you may choose to start enforcing a variety of boundaries all at once, or you may find it easier to start with a couple of simpler ones. Either way, pay close attention to how they impact your daily workflow over the first few weeks. Are the boundaries reducing work-related stress? Are they freeing up your time? Have any conflicts arisen? Use this information to continually assess and adjust your boundaries as needed. You may find it helpful to place a reminder on your calendar now to encourage yourself to reassess in about a month.

Once you've created and enforced your first boundary, you'll have a better idea of how to proceed when it comes time to create more. It will become easier to determine which methods of enforcement work best. Seeing the positive impact from sticking to your boundaries can also be a big help in encouraging you to continue advocating for yourself.

Recapping chapter four

In this chapter, we discussed setting boundaries and enforcing them internally. Below are some of the biggest takeaways:

- Setting boundaries refers to placing limits on what you are willing to do.

- Benefits of setting and enforcing boundaries include stress reduction, increased productivity, strengthened mutual respect with coworkers, and reduced long-term conflict.

- Boundaries can typically be categorized in four ways: mental, physical, personal, and procedural.

- When setting your boundaries, plan for flexibility. Consider if and when exceptions should be made, and write these out as specifically as possible.

- Give yourself grace if you slip up in enforcing your own boundaries, but also use this as an opportunity to brainstorm creative solutions to make the boundaries more doable.

Now that we've established how to set and enforce boundaries with ourselves, we will explore when and how to communicate them to others, and how to navigate any potential related conflicts that may arise.

5

COMMUNICATING BOUNDARIES AND NAVIGATING CONFLICT

"You have to love and respect yourself enough to not let people use and abuse you. You have to set boundaries and keep them, let people clearly know how you won't tolerate to be treated, and let them know how you expect to be treated."

—Jeanette Coron, author

Mastering your story

STICKING TO YOUR OWN boundaries can be challenging on its own, and a new layer of difficulty is added once other people are involved—enforcing them with both yourself and others will require firm confidence.

"Mastering your story" refers to getting (and staying) clear about exactly why you've made specific decisions. In the context of boundaries, this will require you to first come back to the "why" behind your decision to quiet quit. Keep this in mind as your guiding light.

Next, consider how to frame your boundaries in a positive light for the purpose of communicating them to others. What benefits will these boundaries bring to your coworkers, boss, customers, or stakeholders? Will turning down certain assignments allow for a deeper focus on other ones? Will working fewer total hours result in greater productivity during the times you do work? Try to think outside of the box to find any and all ways in which your boundaries will positively impact other people.

Note that "mastering your story" should be an authentic practice, not a dishonest one. Similar to the way in which a child may convince their parents to allow them to attend an event by pitching the educational components they'll learn there, the goal here is to highlight the components of our boundaries that will benefit others. This is a key factor in conflict resolution, as it avoids the assumption that your boundaries are detrimental to everyone else.

Communicating your boundaries

Once you feel comfortable with the boundaries you've set, it's time to consider which ones need to be communicated and to whom. Some boundaries, such as mental and physical ones, may not need to be communicated to anyone else at all. However, procedural boundaries will likely need to be communicated to your boss, colleagues, and/or clients—this will help ensure that you're on the same page and that there aren't any surprises related to the ways in which you'll be completing your work.

Go through your list of boundaries and try asking yourself, "What will happen if I do not communicate this to anyone?" For boundaries that you determine will cause confusion or frustration if not communicated, you should start to formulate a plan to tell the people who need to know.

Several factors may influence how you decide to communicate your boundaries. When possible, communicating them in writing—such as via email or direct message—is helpful in providing a fail-safe for you to point back to when enforcing the boundaries later. However, depending on the nature of the boundary and your relationship with the person you're communicating it to, you may decide that a casual conversation is a more natural option.

Regardless of how you decide to deliver the information, do your best to describe the situation fully, clearly, and professionally. While you don't need to divulge why you are quiet quitting, providing some high-level details about why you're implementing specific boundaries can help to reduce pushback. No need to specifically state that you're increasing your boundaries, but firmly describe how you will be completing tasks moving forward and why this will work best.

Circling back to your practice in "mastering your story," frame your news in a positive light when communicating—this helps to reinforce the fact that you are on the same team as your boss and colleagues. Statistically, people respond best to—and better remember—information that sounds positive and helpful.[34] Emphasize the ways in which your new boundaries will increase your productivity and overall performance. If your boundaries involve distancing yourself from work during your time off, assure your team that this will revitalize you and improve your focus during the workday. You may also choose to commit to responding more quickly during working hours as a trade-off for being unavailable during other times.

Navigating potential conflict

While proactively communicating boundaries early can go a long way toward mitigating potential conflict, it is still possible that you'll find yourself in the middle of a tense situation when enforcing them. Preparing yourself to navigate conflict professionally will help to improve the chances of success with sticking to the boundaries you set.

When does conflict most often arise?

The most frequent causes of workplace conflict are unclear expectations for work, lack of communication, poorly defined areas of responsibility, conflicts of interest, changes, and personality differences.[35] Thankfully, the majority of these conflicts can be resolved—or at least effectively managed—through increased communication. While quiet quitting is "quiet" in many regards, this is one area where you will likely benefit from speaking up, at least to an extent. Although it may be tempting to stay silent in an attempt to avoid conflict altogether, conflicts are typically made significantly worse when they are avoided as opposed to when they are directly dealt with.[36]

Boundary-related conflict can arise anywhere, but it is most prevalent in industries such as banking or nursing, where workers statistically take their work most seriously.[37] Colleagues may feel that you choosing to work less and turn down additional tasks means that you don't care enough about your job. Or, they may feel resentful if they find themselves overworked while you're managing to maintain a healthy work-life balance.

Preparing for difficult conversations

If you find that the boundaries you set seem to be causing annoyance or confusion at work, start by considering the pros and cons of engaging in a conversation as an attempt to resolve it. While communicating is most often a good choice, there are times when it is unnecessary. For instance, if the only conflict is that your colleagues are gossiping about you, it may be simpler to avoid putting additional energy into engaging with them. However, if the conflict is affecting your work or weighing on your conscience, it will likely be best for you to address it.

Once you decide to address conflict head-on, the following guidelines can help you prepare for a successful conversation.[38]

- Focus on the big picture. While it's fine to point out a single instance when someone disrespects a clear boundary, it is more effective to showcase patterns of behavior. Prior to the conversation, try to document the number of times your boss asked you to stay late or your coworker asked for assistance during the times you specifically stated you were unavailable. This allows you to come in armed with data to back up your claims.

* Sit down ahead of time and list out any points you want to be sure to include in the conversation. Focus on highlighting any positives associated with the boundary, such as any increased productivity it has brought.

* Categorize the intensity of the conflict. Use a scale from one to five, where level one is a simple and easily resolved difference, and level five is a deep polarization which leaves little room for resolution.[39] This categorization can help you to choose the best avenue for your conversation. A level one difference can likely be resolved in a casual environment, such as over coffee. Level three conflicts should generally take place in controlled, private, neutral environments with adequate preparation time (and cool-down time) for both parties. A level five conflict may not be resolvable on an individual level and may require intervention from a professional or supervisor.

Addressing the conflict

Once you've adequately prepared, it's time to start the conversation. The following guidelines can help this process go as smoothly as possible.

* Keep communication clear. While it can be tempting to use "softening" statements, offer compliments, or use an overly friendly tone of voice; these behaviors are shown to often backfire, as they can make the other party feel misled, manipulated, or confused.[40] Instead, it's best to use clear statements, beginning with "I" when possible. Clarity makes a favorable resolution more likely in the long term.

* Remain professional. In most cases, it is best not to use humor or inside jokes during a difficult conversation. Insults and personal attacks should always be avoided as well. Don't place blame or purposely use nonverbal clues to try to convey your

opinion. Keep the topic focused on the issue at hand and remain as calm as possible.

- Listen and try to understand the viewpoints of the others in the conversation. Ask open-ended questions when possible. If the other party is behaving irrationally, your instinct may be to dismiss what they are saying—try instead to figure out the underlying cause of their anger. If the conversation gets particularly heated, it may be helpful to suggest postponing it. Conflicts can only be resolved when both parties are willing to listen.

- Look for points of similarity and offer solutions based on those. Aim for statements such as, "Since we both agree this upcoming report is particularly important, I suggest we do x, y, and z to make sure the work gets done in the time that we can both offer. What do you think?" The more you can offer solutions that acknowledge the other person's best interest, the more likely you are to find resolution.

- Stay open to feedback. In the case that someone presents a solid argument as to specifically how your boundary is hurting an aspect of your work, it's okay to ask for some time to reassess as you consider whether your boundaries can be adjusted to better meet the needs of both parties.

- Always end by recapping the solutions you've agreed on. Ensure the other person is on the same page, and then write the solutions somewhere you can both access—an email or a shared document are great options.

If the same topic comes up again, refer back to the written solutions. While circumstances may change—requiring new discussion—your agreed-upon solutions can act as a starting point in the future.

Recapping chapter five

This chapter explored how to positively frame your boundaries, communicate them with others, and navigate conflict. Takeaways are included below.

- Master your story by authentically determining the ways in which your boundaries will benefit the people you work with.

- Consider who you will need to communicate your boundaries to. Deliver the information clearly, professionally, and in a positive light.

- When addressing conflict, adequately prepare yourself to engage in the conversation. Focus on the big picture and highlight positive points where possible.

- Increase the chances of a favorable outcome from a conflict conversation by listening to understand and looking for points of similarity. Recap agreed-upon solutions at the end.

Next, we will dive into ways to increase efficiency to further maximize your time, making it easier to stick to your boundaries in the long-term.

6

IMPLEMENTING STRATEGIES FOR INCREASED EFFICIENCY

"Workaholics aren't heroes. They don't save the day, they just use it up. The real hero is home because they figured out a faster way."

—Jason Fried, CEO of Basecamp

What does it mean to work smarter?

YOU'VE LIKELY HEARD THE phrase "work smarter, not harder" thrown around in a variety of settings. But what does this mean in practice?

Working smarter encompasses a wide variety of tactics—from bigger overarching "hacks" like creating templates for common tasks you need to complete, to simpler tactics like keeping organized notes you can easily come back to reference. This chapter will break down six different categories of strategies, each designed to help you work more efficiently:

- **Organization:** Learn how to organize your time, to-do list, and workspace while streamlining everyday tasks.

- **Automation:** Explore a few of the ways you may be able to use artificial intelligence and simple programming to automate frequent processes.

- **Prioritization:** Discover simple strategies to guide you in determining the best order in which to tackle the tasks on your plate.

- **Delegation:** Understand when and how you may be able to delegate tasks.

- **Understanding "good enough":** Challenge perfectionist tendencies and learn how to decide when a project is complete.

- **Saying "no":** Determine when it is appropriate and beneficial to say "no," and how you can go about doing so.

Reducing your workload is the entire point of quiet quitting, so finding time-saving strategies that work for you will be key. It is likely that some of the strategies shared here may make sense to use in your situation while others may not, so you may find it helpful to take note of the ones that stand out to you.

Finding your optimal organizational systems

Organization can feel like a loaded topic, as it encompasses such a wide range. Thinking about trying to organize meetings, tasks, and notes can easily lead to overwhelm—how do you choose where to start? This section will walk through strategies to organize your time, your to-do list, and your physical space. And lastly, we'll look at how to streamline the simple everyday tasks that can add up to be bigger distractions.

Organizing your time

One of the biggest benefits of building an organizational system is taking things off your mental load. If you're mentally keeping track of your upcoming meetings, events, and time-bound tasks—even if this strategy is working well and you never mix up a date or time—you could likely benefit from freeing up this space in your brain. Having everything written on a calendar not only allows you to see upcoming events at a glance, but it also enables you to easily share details with others when needed.

While physical pen-and-paper calendars and planners are better than nothing, digital calendars will save you more time and give you more flexibility. Here are some reasons to consider an online cloud-based calendar.

- Easily sync between devices, allowing you to access and edit your calendar from anywhere.

- Quickly schedule reoccurrences with a few clicks.

- Include all relevant details, including links, photos, and addresses.

- Share upcoming events with others as needed—you can share as much or as little detail as you like.

- If applicable, use your calendar as a way to block-out chunks of time; tags such as "out of office" can easily signal to coworkers that you are unavailable.

- Search your entire calendar—past and future—quickly without flipping through pages.

- Sync with Apple Maps or Google Maps, allowing your device to automatically remind you when it's time to leave to get to your next destination on time.

- Automate many processes (which we'll dive deeper into in the next section).

If you decide to use a cloud-based calendar, you'll have several good options to choose from. Top choices that allow for a large variety of features and integrations include Microsoft (Outlook), Google, and Apple. Calendars can be synced between these three platforms, so don't worry too much about picking the "best" one. Simply create a free account through any of these three companies (or log in using an existing account) and start dropping your upcoming appointments into the calendar. Then, log into the same account on your other devices to ensure you can access the details from anywhere. This will help to keep you both up-to-date and accountable while freeing up your mental resources to focus elsewhere.

Organizing your to-do list

For some people, to-do lists feel daunting due to the seemingly never-ending number of tasks. However, as mentioned in chapter two, getting these tasks onto paper (or a screen) can greatly reduce mental load and set you on a path toward lowering your stress levels.

Again, a digital system will give you more functionality than pen and paper. There are many to-do list apps available, so you can certainly be picky about choosing one with features that work best for you. A few options are Asana, Monday.com, Trello, and Microsoft To Do. Once you choose a system, take a bit of time to learn its capabilities. Many systems have built-in tutorials, but YouTube videos can also be a big help if you get stuck.

So how can you organize your to-do list to minimize overwhelm? The specifics will depend on your unique needs, but finding ways to categorize and prioritize tasks will be key. You may choose to categorize by type of task, associated project, location, or any other factor that makes sense to you. It can also be helpful to include details for tasks, including any due dates or relevant links. The upcoming section on strategic prioritization will provide further insight into taking your to-do list to the next level through prioritization.

Next, you'll need to turn your system into a habit. While this may not happen overnight, it's a crucial part of the optimization process. If needed, you can start by setting reminders for yourself to check and update your to-do list throughout the day. Don't be afraid to continuously analyze and adjust your system to best meet your needs. Perhaps you'll find that adding tasks at the beginning of each day works best, or maybe you'll prefer updating it as you wind down before bed. Either way, staying flexible to adding additional tasks on the fly is also helpful.

Keeping your list easily accessible is particularly important. This may sound counterintuitive, as much of quiet quitting revolves around separating work and personal life. However, if you're laying down to sleep and remember an important task, you should be able to write it down immediately—this actually supports your work-life balance by allowing you to fully dismiss the thought from your mind. If you need to remember that task until you're back at work, it will add to your mental load and may negatively impact your ability to enjoy life outside of work.

Once your system is in place, you can begin to reap the benefits. If you find yourself thinking about the work you need to do or mentally planning your next day, remind yourself, "I don't need to think about this; it's written on my list." This is particularly essential, as the only way to truly reduce your mental load is to rely on the organizational system you worked hard to structure.

Organizing your workspace

When living or working in a messy space, your brain spends valuable resources trying to make sense of the environment or find things that aren't in their proper place. While you may not have full control over your workspace, there are steps you can take to increase organization and improve usability.

If you have a dedicated physical workspace—whether it's an office, a desk, or even a car or another unique environment—that is exclusively used by you, then you can take full ownership over finding a system that works best for you. While every job and every person may vary in the type of space they will thrive in, here are a few tips to consider.

- Go through every item in your workspace and remove the ones that serve no purpose. For items meant to bring joy or personality to the space—such as photos of your family or your favorite collectibles—consider whether the items serve as more of a positive force or a distraction.

- Consider which items you utilize for work on a regular basis and ensure they are easily accessible. Depending on the volume, you may want to consider adding a filing cabinet, storage drawers, or color-coordinated folders to the mix.

- Confining and labeling items can go a long way toward ensuring long-term organization. This helps define where new items should go, and it also trains your brain to come back to the correct spot to find them.

If you share your workspace with others, you may not have full control over the area, but you can still implement strategies to help your own items stay organized. One helpful strategy is to find a space that *is* exclusively yours—perhaps a locker at your worksite or a bag you can bring with you daily—and focus on fully organizing that. You can follow the same tips above to ensure that your smaller space stays in order. Then, upon starting work each day, consider taking a few extra moments to familiarize yourself with the setup of your space that day. Taking extra time to set up your space may seem like a waste, but it can actually end up saving you a significant amount of time throughout the day.

If the space you work in is constantly changing—such as if you travel frequently—these same tips apply. Find a bag or suitcase where you can organize everything you'll need for quick, easy access.

Lastly—if any of your work is done on a computer, phone, or tablet—consider the organization of your digital workspace as well.

- Set aside time to sort your files into folders and sub-folders. This doesn't have to be done all at once, but it is an important part of your organizational system. You may choose to organize by project, customer, date, file type, or an entirely different way depending on your job functions. Think about what makes the most sense for you, and don't be afraid to adjust the system as your duties and priorities change.

- If possible, back your files up to the cloud. This ensures that your organizational system is accessible from anywhere, saving you time by avoiding processes like emailing yourself the latest version of each document. It also allows you to share files more quickly and seamlessly if needed.

- Create folders for your email, and sort messages accordingly. Programs such as Microsoft Outlook can even be programmed to sort mail automatically, saving you additional time. Be sure that your system prioritizes highlighting the emails that you need to follow up on to ensure they are not lost in the mix. You can create a "follow-up" email folder, mark the messages as unread until they're addressed, or use a flagging process.

- Consider creating a virtual notebook where you can keep information you need to reference regularly. Having this information virtually, as opposed to keeping it in a paper notebook, will give you the benefits of being able to quickly search, reorganize, and copy data. Microsoft OneNote and Evernote are two options you can utilize for this functionality.

It may take some trial and error to find the organizational systems that work best for you. Continue to pay close attention to what's working and what isn't. If you find yourself searching for an item—either physically or digitally—consider where you can place that item for easier access in the future.

Streamlining everyday tasks

Finally, you can utilize simple routines to streamline everyday tasks and save yourself even more time and mental capacity.

Think about all the small, seemingly straightforward, and insignificant tasks you encounter throughout the day. Some examples include:

- Picking your clothing for the day

- Choosing what to have for breakfast

- Making or ordering your lunch

- Finding your keys, phone, wallet, or any other necessary items

When these tasks are not streamlined, the energy spent on them can add to your stress and mental load. Conversely, you can use organization and preparation to make these types of tasks more effortless in the moment, allowing you to focus on things that matter more.

Again, the best specific solutions will vary by person, but here are a few suggestions to consider trying.

- When doing laundry, pre-plan your outfits for each day of the week and set them in defined spaces.

- Meal prep ahead of time, or thoroughly plan for the food you'll make and set out the ingredients you'll need.

- Place any food orders ahead of time with scheduled delivery. If you're unable to do this due to an unpredictable schedule, you can at least look at the menu ahead of time to speed up your order in the moment.

- Create a space where your essentials—keys, wallet, etc.—stay when not in use. You can also consider adding a tracking device, such as Tile or AirTag, to these items if you tend to misplace them frequently.

As you begin to implement organizational solutions, you should find yourself focusing less time and energy on trivial decisions and tasks. To make these processes even easier on an everyday basis, many systems can be automated so that you can truly "set and forget." We'll take a look at strategies for automation next.

Utilizing technology to automate your processes

Automating processes can help save you time in many areas. Here, we'll walk through a few options for automating aspects of some of the most common workplace tasks. Due to the incredibly vast number of options, we won't be able to dive into deep detail, but a wide breadth of tutorials are available for each of the programs and features mentioned—typically, a YouTube search is a great place to start for finding comprehensive how-to videos for free.

As you read, you may find it helpful to take note of options that would benefit you. While this section cannot cover every scenario, you can also use this as a starting point to brainstorm and research more specialized strategies for your industry. If the ideas mentioned here don't quite match up with the types of tasks you work on, you can try Google searching "automating tasks for" with your industry, job title, or specific type of work. Or—for a highly customized solution without the work of figuring out and setting up a process—you may also choose to consider hiring someone on Fiverr or Upwork to assist you in automating your tasks.

Automating data entry

If you spend any portion of your week filling in forms or spreadsheets, copying and pasting information, or messaging details to a colleague, you can likely find ways to speed up these processes and free up more of your time. This can also help you avoid the monotonous and frustrating feeling often experienced with repetitive time-consuming tasks.

Zapier, Outfunnel, Leadsbridge, IFTTT, and Microsoft Power Automate are a few of the more robust programs that allow you to automate many aspects of your work—from automatically messaging your boss when you receive a lead to automatically creating calendar events when a form is completed. While these programs will have a bit of a learning curve, they do not require any coding or specialized skills.

If setting up these advanced functions sounds too overwhelming right now, you may choose to start with simpler automation, such as creating a form that automatically fills in a spreadsheet for you. Microsoft Forms and Google Forms are two free options for this functionality. You can further utilize Microsoft Excel or Google Sheets to sort and manipulate data quickly.

Managing your email with automation

In the organization section, we discussed creating folders to organize your email inbox. Automation allows you to take this process a step further, saving the hassle of manually marking and sorting each message.

Microsoft Outlook offers a robust set of features that allow you to "set and forget" your email organization. Using rules, you can specify that all messages from a certain client go to a certain folder, or you can automatically flag all messages you receive from your boss. You can even automatically delete messages from a particular address to save time wading through spam. Further, you can utilize quick steps to create one-click functionality, such as simultaneously marking an item as read, moving it to a specified folder, and creating a calendar event.

If you'd prefer to stick with a web-based email experience (such as gmail.com or outlook.com) or if you're primarily using your phone for email, you can utilize third-party add-ons to gain automation functionality. As an example, Boomerang is a program available on each of these platforms which allows you to schedule emails to send later, track responses, and set reminders.

Consider which parts of email management take the greatest amount of your time and energy, and try searching for automation solutions. It's likely that there are a variety of ways you can streamline these tasks.

Automating social media posts

If your job involves posting to social media, there are a number of services you can utilize to schedule your posts ahead of time, see engagement statistics at a glance, and create templates to speed up the creation of on-brand content. Hootsuite, StoryChief, and Canva are a few of the most popular programs you can explore to simplify your content creation.

Creating a posting schedule allows you to curate content in more focused blocks of time, then freeing you up to focus on other aspects of your job the rest of the time. Generally, working on similar tasks all at once maximizes your time since you spend less energy switching back and forth between various setups and mindsets.

Using technology to assist with writing and editing

If your job involves any amount of writing or proofreading—whether it's sending emails, drafting reports, creating presentations, or something else—you can likely benefit from utilizing technology to help you.

Tools like Grammarly and ProWritingAid can be installed on your device to automatically scan text you write and give you real-time suggestions to improve readability and professionalism. While most programs already include a built-in spell checker, these tools give more advanced advice that can save you time stressing over the best ways to convey your thoughts.

Artificial intelligence tools such as ChatGPT and Microsoft Copilot also have functionalities that can assist with your writing. You can ask these chatbots to provide feedback or summarization of your text, or use them to find sources to reference as you research a topic.

Before utilizing these tools, make sure to double-check whether your employer has any restrictions on AI use. And remember, while AI can be a useful tool to assist with your writing, it shouldn't replace the personal touch you bring to your work.

Brainstorming and planning with AI

Artificial intelligence is helpful for more than just writing, too. You can utilize these same tools to help you brainstorm ideas, answer questions, or create an outline for a project. You may even try asking AI for ideas on how to automate your work!

Again, be sure to verify that you're not violating any employer policies with your use of AI. It's also a best practice to verify the information you receive through AI, as these tools are still developing and do not always give perfect responses.

Getting started with automation

Automating your workflow may feel overwhelming at first, but it can also bring some of the biggest rewards in time and energy saved long-term. Below are a few ways to mitigate stress while beginning your automation journey.

- Make a list of repetitive tasks you do often. Then, try searching for ways to automate parts of them. Prioritize finding solutions for tasks that take up the most time.

- Start simple, by experimenting with automating small parts of your workflow. Over time, as you get more comfortable with the programs you're using, you can build up to more complex automation.

- Explore what automation options are available within the programs you're already using. This can help save time by avoiding a learning curve and may also save money by avoiding paying for multiple services.

- Compare different programs to see which options will best meet your needs. (You can even ask AI to help you with this!) Many systems offer free versions or free trials, allowing you to test them firsthand.

- Always test your automations to verify they work the way you're intending. The last thing you want is to end up with the wrong emails auto-deleting or a post sharing to the wrong account.

Experimenting with automation—even if technology feels unfamiliar or daunting—can significantly reduce your workload and maximize your time each day. Start small and, once you start to gain comfort and familiarity, try expanding your automation further.

Strategic prioritization

Figuring out which tasks to complete at which time can be another factor adding to your mental load. Without a strong prioritization system, it's easy to get tunnel vision and end up dedicating hours to completing tasks that ultimately are neither important nor urgent.

Building your Eisenhower matrix

So, how can you avoid the traps of poor prioritization? A great place to start is with making a list of all the tasks on your plate. (If you've already created a to-do list, you can simply reference that, adding to it as needed.) Make sure to include everything from the most minimal tasks—such as submitting reports and sending reminders to colleagues—to the crucial and daunting ones. Tangential tasks, such as committee involvement or researching new industry trends, should be listed as well.

Next, categorize tasks by importance and urgency using an Eisenhower matrix. President Dwight D. Eisenhower explained the importance of this, stating, "By organizing tasks by both urgency and importance, this tool guides you to the tasks that need to be finished the soonest."[41]

This activity can be done digitally—perhaps within your online notebook—or physically with pen and paper. The matrix should include four boxes, allowing you to categorize tasks by importance and urgency. A blank Eisenhower matrix looks like this:

Important, but not urgent	**Urgent and important**
Not urgent and not important	**Urgent, but not important**

Once you've created the matrix, place each task on your list into the box where it fits best. If you find yourself struggling to decide which tasks are important or urgent, keep these guidelines in mind.

- A task is *important* when not completing it will have a major impact—on your work, your company, or your standing in your job. For the purpose of this exercise, tasks that must be completed but do not require any specialized skills or knowledge should be considered unimportant.

- A task is *urgent* when it has an immediate impact, is unavoidable, and/or must be completed within a certain period of time. (The exact period of time that qualifies a task as urgent can vary quite a bit depending on your role and duties. You may need to choose where to draw the line, such as one day or one week.)

An important and urgent task could be submitting a quarterly report to your supervisor. If you fail to complete this type of task, it may lead to negative consequences with your boss. Since these types of reports are timely, they are also likely to have strict deadlines when they must be submitted.

An important but not urgent task may be reaching out to potential new clients. This type of task can benefit your work, but it most likely does not need to be done immediately.

An urgent but unimportant task might be cataloguing invoices from last quarter. This needs to be done soon, but it doesn't require specific skills to do well.

Finally, an unimportant and not urgent task could be reorganizing a database. Unless the current database isn't functioning properly, improving it could be useful, but it isn't urgent and it likely won't have a big impact on your work.

Below is an example of an Eisenhower matrix filled in with a few examples. Keep in mind that you may categorize the same types of tasks differently—all roles are different and will require different prioritization. The key is to consider the impact each task will have on your work and to categorize accordingly. You can always re-categorize tasks later, so don't worry too much about perfectly placing them on your first try.

Important, but not urgent	Urgent and important
• Staying up to date with industry trends • Networking • Outreaching to potential new clients	• Replying to emails from boss or important clients • Responding to crises • Meeting major financial deadlines
Not urgent and not important	**Urgent, but not important**
• Updating functional parts of work • Reading every single email • Attending meetings unrelated to your work	• Responding to requests from coworkers • Filling out forms • Compiling information or data

Once you've arranged your tasks into the matrix, it's time to determine how to proceed with each category of tasks. Below are base recommendations to consider:

Important, but not urgent **Decide**	Urgent and important **Do**
Not urgent and not important **Delete**	Urgent, but not important **Delegate**

Do: Tasks that are both important and urgent should jump to the top of your to-do list when possible.

Delegate: Tasks that are urgent but not important often don't require specialized skills to complete, so finding ways to delegate or automate as many of these tasks as possible can help to free up your time.

Decide: Tasks that are important but not urgent are often continually pushed aside in favor of more urgent tasks, in which case re-prioritization may be needed to ensure they're not ignored forever. Consider if there are ways to break these tasks up into smaller, more easily doable parts—perhaps parts can even be automated or delegated. You may also find it helpful to associate your own goals or deadlines with these tasks to increase their urgency.

Delete: Generally, most tasks that are neither urgent nor important simply do not need to be done. Take a look at the tasks you placed into this section—would there be any negative impact from deleting them? For the tasks where "deleting" is not possible, such as a mandatory meeting unrelated to your work, consider if there is anything you can do to minimize the task's negative impact while maximizing its positive impact. During the meeting, for example, perhaps you can find time to network (helping toward an important but not urgent goal) or socialize (likely not directly impacting your work, but contributing to boosting your morale).

Note that any personal tasks—grabbing your morning coffee, catching up with coworkers, checking in with family throughout the day—should not be "deleted" if they are important to you and helping to maintain your work-life balance. Consider building short breaks into your schedule to complete these so they are less likely to directly interfere with your productivity.

Daily prioritized to-do lists with the 1-3-6 principle

After making any needed adjustments to your Eisenhower matrix, you'll be ready to create a prioritized version of your to-do list using the 1-3-6 principle. This strategy will help you build a plan of attack for your next workday.

At the top of your list, place **one urgent and important task**. Placing only one may seem counterintuitive, as many people want to complete all important and urgent tasks first. This may be necessary in some situations, but urgent and important tasks are often both mentally draining and time consuming, so packing your list with them unnecessarily may leave you feeling overworked while also not giving you adequate time for other tasks. Instead, aim to complete one each day, adding to this only when truly necessary. Completing the urgent and important task first thing in the morning works best for many people, as it allows ample time to ensure the task is not rushed. However, if you know you're more mentally focused after lunch, it may make more sense to block time for this task in the afternoon. Paying attention to what works best for you and continuously adjusting your strategy will help to maximize you r efficiency.

Next, place **three important but not urgent tasks** onto your list. These tasks are generally less mentally draining, as you won't feel rushed to meet a deadline. You may choose to start working on a task that will eventually become urgent, such as a report that isn't due for another month, to get ahead of last-minute stress. You may also add tasks that have no real deadline, such as responding to non-urgent emails, creating general social media posts, or outreaching to new clients. When considering exactly how to add these tasks to your daily to-do list, it's helpful to set attainable goals—even ones that feel too easy—as you can always decide to do more if time allows. Rather than shooting to connect with 20 new clients, maybe you consider aiming to connect with five. Rather than setting out to reply to every email, set an attainable number and leave any other non-urgent messages for the next day.

Finally, add **six urgent but unimportant tasks** to your list. If six sounds like an overwhelming number, take a moment to consider the mental load of these particular tasks. Typically, this is a primary type of task that will be automated or delegated, so many of them should be quicker and easier on your end. Perhaps you'll fill out a form with an automated tool, ask a colleague to follow up on an email addressed to both of you, and check on the progress of a task with another coworker—this is three tasks completed already.

Here's an example of a to-do list for an office job, crafted with the 1-3-6 principle:

- 1: Prepare the presentation for the director's meeting tomorrow

- 3: Reach out to five potential new clients

- 3: Craft a post for LinkedIn

- 3: Schedule next week's meetings

- 6: Attend the managers' meeting

- 6: Ask Joe to gather initial figures for the final report

- 6: Confirm whether Ella has finished editing the quarterly report

- 6: Run a program you've set up to clear out unneeded emails

- 6: Reply to the email from Mark

- 6: Fill out the form for last week's new hire from the template

Once your list is complete, try working through it top to bottom on your next workday. With less important tasks scheduled toward the end of the day, you're less likely to feel the need to stay late. Throughout the day, adjust as needed and shift tasks to tomorrow's list if necessary. You may also choose to have a dedicated time at the end of each day to assess the day's work and create tomorrow's prioritized list.

Lastly, it can be helpful to come back to the Eisenhower matrix activity every 2-3 months. (Perhaps, place a reminder on your calendar now so you don't forget.) It's normal for everyday tasks to change in priority, and this exercise can be a good way to reassess where you are focusing your energy. Look for tasks that can be moved from "do" or "decide"—can any more of these be automated or delegated? Can any more tasks be deleted altogether? These types of shifts will help to streamline your focus during your workday, enabling you to live a fuller life while still providing value to your company.

When to delegate

For many people, delegation can be one of the most difficult strategies to implement. It's easy to feel like you need to do everything yourself in order for it to be done correctly. However, unsurprisingly, trying to take on all tasks without assistance can easily lead to overload.

As mentioned in the previous section, tasks that are urgent but not particularly important are often good candidates to consider for delegation. Here are a few additional considerations to help you determine whether to delegate a task:

- **Does the task absolutely need to be done?** Even a delegated task requires some degree of oversight and follow-up, so if you can take the task off your plate entirely, this is better than delegating it.

- **Can the task be automated?** If automation is an option, this is likely easier than delegating, as it doesn't require you to coordinate with anyone else.

- **Is there someone else who can do this task?** Some tasks are unable to be delegated because they require your unique experience, skills, or training. Others may not be able to be delegated for compliance reasons—if you are required to sign off on a task, ensure you fully understand the implications of potential delegation.

- **What is your plan for follow-up?** Most delegated tasks will require some form of follow-up. Ensure that your plan for following up isn't more time consuming than it would be to simply complete the task yourself.

If you determine that a task can be delegated, the next step is to choose who to delegate to. If you're a people manager with direct reports, you may already have someone in mind. If not, it may feel trickier figuring out how to ask for assistance.

One way to make delegation easier is to look for ways that it can be mutually beneficial for you and the person you're asking. This could mean working with a peer to shuffle around assignments, with you taking on more of their administrative work (which you'll use automation to help speed up) and them taking on some of your outreach. Or, it could mean coordinating with a colleague so that you each attend a specific meeting every-other week and share notes with each other, freeing up extra time for each of you. Asking your coworkers what types of tasks are overwhelming them may help you determine ways in which you can help each other to succeed.

Lastly, look for any tasks you're currently doing that should be falling to another team. Are you frequently assisting your team with technical questions which could instead be delegated to a dedicated IT department? Are you pulled into conversations to translate for other team members? Taking even small tasks like these off your plate can help to reduce your mental load significantly.

Is "good enough" good enough?

In today's society, many people see perfection as the ultimate goal. In some cases, this makes sense. When your product or service will have a wide reach, it is essential for it to be high quality and well fleshed out. However, in many cases, the everyday work we're completing really can be just "good enough."

For instance, I have struggled for long periods of time over the right wording of a sentence in an email that will only go to one or two people. Any of the eight ways I reworded that sentence would have gotten my point across just fine, and the recipients never would have cared any differently. In most cases, no one else will notice that a color may have looked a little better if it were a shade lighter, and no one will think twice about you signing off your email with "best regards" instead of "sincerely"—or vice versa.

To be clear, this isn't to say that projects should be done lazily without regard for meeting essential requirements. Projects that are truly unfinished should *not* be dismissed as "good enough." However, there's a very wide range between unfinished and perfect—and often, much of that range is acceptable.

So, how can you determine when a product is "good enough?" If you find yourself continuing to work on something that may be ready to hand in, consider asking yourself the following three questions.

- **Does this meet the minimum requirements?** If you're unsure, reference any written policies, procedures, templates, or directions. You can also ask your boss or peer for a sample to compare to.

- **Will it make sense to the recipient or customer?** Try to look at your product through fresh eyes. If you can, set the project aside and come back to reassess it later. As long as it makes sense, it is likely good to go. You can also choose to ask a colleague to look over your work and let you know if they are confused about anything.

- **Do I find it acceptable?** Remember that any work you produce will be associated with you, so it's important not to cut corners. That said, try to keep realistically low standards—aim for work that is acceptable enough to meet all requirements without too much extra work above and beyond that.

If you answer yes to all three questions, consider the project complete, turn it in, and move on.

Understanding perfectionism

If the thought of moving on from any project before it's perfect feels stressful, you may be struggling with perfectionism. While this quality is likely to help you achieve greater success with larger projects that really matter, it can also hold you back by increasing your workload and making even the smallest insignificant tasks feel unmanageable.

Perfectionism comes from three main sources. The first is personal-standards perfectionism, which you may experience if you feel intrinsically drawn to complete work perfectly. This type of perfectionism is less likely to directly cause burnout, but it can still lead to overwhelm due to projects taking longer and work piling up. And further, it may not actually be what's best for your work either—if you're focusing more time and energy perfecting minor aspects that truly don't matter, you have less to spend on more important tasks. If you believe you're experiencing personal-standards perfectionism, try reflecting on the pros and cons of this approach. This will give you a solid foundation to understand whether perfectionism is doing more harm or good in your unique situation.

A second type of perfectionism is self-critical perfectionism. People who experience this often feel that they are never good enough to achieve their goals. These people may push and push to perfect a project, only to end up frustrated with their own results. If this resonates with you, try setting small, specific, and manageable goals for your work to let yourself know when you've done "enough." You may even set a maximum amount of time you'll allow yourself to spend on a certain project or task. Once you've met your goals, remind yourself that you've done all you set out to do and that there's no need to push for more. While this may be easier said than done, continually practicing it will help it become second nature in time.

The final type of perfectionism is socially driven. Perhaps you work in an industry where standards are high, or perhaps you grew up in a family where perfection was expected at all times. If you feel this type of outside pressure to be perfect, try to redefine your attitude toward work, revolving around the factors that are meaningful to you. It may help to maintain a list of things you are good at and enjoy—both inside and outside of the workplace—that you can consult when you feel pressure to do one specific thing well. If you feel comfortable to do so, it may also help to have targeted conversations with people you feel pressure from. It is likely that these people may not know the pressure they're creating, and clearing the air may help to both improve your relationship and diffuse the pressure.

The key to working "good enough" is to continually hold yourself accountable for delivering on the elements and projects that matter while allowing yourself to let go of the rest. Keep in mind that, depending on your job, this could be ever-changing—you'll need to continue to assess your position's goals and expectations, adjusting accordingly. If you struggle with knowing when to move on from tasks, try creating guidelines for yourself and sticking to them. It may take some trial and error, but finding ways to fight perfectionism while delivering on all minimum requirements is essential to a creating a balanced life.

Saying "no"

At work, many of us often find ourselves taking on more tasks than we realistically need to. Maybe you attend optional meetings or help coworkers with tasks outside of your job description. Perhaps, when your boss asks if you can take on one more little thing, you feel you have to say "yes."

What would happen if you, instead, said "no" in each of these scenarios?

The answer to this question may not be completely straightforward. Perhaps some of the "extra" tasks you take on have a positive impact that make them worthwhile to you. If this is the case, you can always mindfully make the decision to answer "yes." However, finding comfort in defaulting to "no" is where your power comes in. It may be difficult at first—especially if you've built a track record of never turning down extra work. But the good news is that, generally, the more often you start saying "no," the easier it will get.

Before answering any requests, take a brief moment to consider the facts.

- Is it related to a direct, core function of your job?

- Is the request reasonable?

- Do you have the capacity?

When the answer to any of these questions is no, respectfully yet firmly decline.

Sometimes, the hardest part of saying no is sticking with your decision afterwards. If you find yourself struggling with this, try addressing it within the boundaries you set for yourself.

Recapping chapter six

This chapter presented an overview of six categories of strategies designed to help you work more efficiently—organization, automation, prioritization, delegation, knowing when something is "good enough," and saying "no." While it may not be possible to utilize all of these strategies in your work, use this as a starting point to brainstorm ways to streamline your own tasks. Below are some general guidelines to keep in mind.

- Setting up a digital calendar is a great way to keep yourself on track while also providing a basis for automating and streamlining tasks.

- Keeping a well-organized workspace can greatly reduce overwhelm. Both physical and digital workspaces should be considered.

- Many simple tasks can be automated to save you time. If you're unsure where to start, try searching for an automation option for an easy task you do often.

- Categorizing tasks by importance and urgency can help you to create a strategic prioritization plan.

- For tasks that do not require your personal expertise, consider whether delegation is an option.

- Always hold yourself accountable to completing the minimum requirements of a task, but be cautious of putting in too much extra effort on top of that. Check in with yourself often to see if a project is realistically "good enough" to be considered complete.

- Stay mindful of any work you're taking on that goes above and beyond your job description. Don't be afraid to say "no" and hold your ground when a request is not reasonable.

If you're still not sure where to start, ask yourself what would make your work life easier. What are your most time-consuming tasks? What frustrates you the most? What often keeps you at work late? What do you find yourself doing over and over? What feels like a waste of time? What do you often forget?

Choose a problem you want to tackle and begin implementing potential solutions. It may take some trial and error to find the ideal ways to streamline your tasks, so stick with it and don't be afraid to continually adjust.

Next, we'll explore what happens after you successfully quiet quit—how can you ensure that this decision is worthwhile and effectively contributes to a fuller life?

7

Capitalizing on New Opportunities

"I have looked in the mirror every morning and asked myself: 'If today were the last day of my life, would I want to do what I am about to do today?' And whenever the answer has been 'No' for too many days in a row, I know I need to change something."
—Steve Jobs, co-founder and former CEO of Apple

Reaping the benefits of quiet quitting

SUCCESSFULLY IMPROVING YOUR WORK-LIFE balance after quiet quitting is no small feat. Upon reaching this point, you've undoubtedly put a lot of time and effort into finding ways to work more efficiently and enforce the boundaries you need. Finally finding that balance you've been striving for can be incredibly rewarding in itself, but what happens next?

Finding yourself with newfound "free time" can sometimes feel like a new type of overwhelm, with endless possibilities weighing on your desire to make the most of every moment. This chapter aims to arm you with ways to take full advantage of the new opportunities you're presented with.

Maximizing your time with family and friends

The ability to spend more time with family and friends can be highly fulfilling. Most people report a boost in mental health when spending time with those they care about, especially when those people are their friends or their children.[42]

However, increasing the amount of time spent with loved ones doesn't always lead to positive experience. Some people find that time with family can quickly turn to activities with negative associations—such as trying to get children to do chores or having logistical discussions with a spouse.[43] While these types of interactions have their place, it's important to mindfully create quality time focused on more pleasant experiences as well.

One way to foster more positive interactions is to remove yourself (and those you're spending time with) from your usual environments. People have strong associations with places where they spend the most time—home, school, work, etc. Your mind may function in a very specific way within these environments, and it may be easily distracted by the pile of dishes in the sink or the chip in the tile from a child's temper tantrum. And keep in mind that others—even children—likely have similarly strong associations, even if they are unaware of them. At least occasionally, try to plan quality time in new or less frequented locations. Feel free to get creative—you could go outside, to a restaurant, or somewhere more unique such as a zoo or a beach.

Mindfully structuring some of your time with others in another way to increase the likelihood of a positive outcome. Scheduling dedicated time with people and routinely showing up shows that you prioritize the relationship. While some may argue that scheduled time with partners doesn't sound very romantic, setting aside specific time free from distractions can be a great way to create positive experiences.[44] You may choose to structure the time with your loved ones by setting up a regular game night, signing up for weekly cooking classes together, or taking on a shared art project. Structured activities are helpful in taking away pressure to constantly plan new activities, and they allow for your interests to grow alongside your friends and family.

While these tips can provide fun and effective ways to improve your relationships, follow what best suits your unique preferences and goals. If you and your family love spending time together at home, or if you thrive while planning new activities weekly, following these passions is likely the best path.

Prioritizing self-care

Finding additional time to care for yourself is another distinct benefit of quiet quitting. Self-care refers to "a multidimensional, multifaceted process of purposeful engagement in strategies that promote healthy functioning and enhance well-being."[45] People who practice intentional self-care are found to be more resilient, report higher levels of happiness, find themselves with increased energy, and experience less burnout.[46] Self-care can be sorted into five general categories: physical, social, mental, spiritual, and emotional.

- **Physical** self-care includes eating well, sleeping enough, getting movement or exercise, and taking charge of any health conditions you may have.

- **Social** self-care relates to spending time with others. Who you choose to spend time with and how much time you choose to spend will depend on your individual needs.

- **Mental** self-care involves keeping your mind sharp and positive. This may mean reading books, watching movies, doing puzzles, engaging in positive self-talk—anything that improves your mental health.

- **Spiritual** self-care may relate to religion, or it may involve other activities that help you feel connected to the world around you—meditation, walks in nature, or simply spending time alone.

- **Emotional** self-care means processing negative emotions such as stress, anger, and sadness. You may choose to directly think through your feelings, or you may find that dedicating additional time to calming activities helps you to move through the feelings effectively.

When developing a self-care routine, include at least some activities that you are drawn to and that you know you can easily complete. Adding these successes to your routine will make it easier to build more challenging activities on if you choose to do so.

Bringing attention to sleep, exercise, and purpose-building can be particularly beneficial, as these have been shown to have the largest impact on physical and mental health and are even linked to increased lifespan.[47] Purpose-building relates to anything that feels important to you and gives your life purpose. Working toward a meaningful goal or finding ways to give back to others are often found to fill this need.

In the long term, many people find that their mental health is strengthened the most when they are able to prioritize activities from each of the five categories of self-care. This may sound like a lot, but even small activities can make a big impact. For example, you may choose to exercise a few times a week for your physical health, participate in a monthly game night with friends for your social health, carve out a couple of hours a week for a hobby for your mental health, meditate for five minutes a day for your spiritual health, and create a calming bedtime routine for your emotional health.

Seeking new work and professional growth

Regardless of whether professional growth was a key motivator in your decision to quiet quit, you may decide that you'd like to take on some new form of work. Depending on your goals and interests, this could come in several forms. You may consider one or any combination of the following.

- **Look for a new job.** This could be a new full-time job to replace your current one—perhaps the "next step" in your career or a shift to better align with your professional goals and interests. You may also choose to search for part-time work to help build your resume, increase your income, or provide you with additional professional opportunities.

- **Start your own business or "side hustle."** With this path, you get the flexibility to focus on something you're passionate about and decide how much time and energy you want to dedicate to it. You can choose to sell handmade items on Etsy, create a social media platform for a cause you care about, or build a new business from the ground up.

- **Offer freelance services.** This is another opportunity to set your own schedule and parameters. Websites like Upwork and Fiverr can help you get started quickly, matching your skill sets with the needs of businesses and individuals.

- **Volunteer.** This can be a unique way to gain experience, find purpose, build connections, and exercise your passions.

If you do decide to take on new work, consider ways to implement similar time-saving and boundary-enforcing strategies from the start. Define exactly what you're willing to do and when you're willing to do it. Automate and delegate when you can. Communicate your needs early with anyone involved. For remote work, consider whether it would be helpful to have a specific space to work from—whether that's a defined corner of your home, a coworking space, or a coffee shop—to keep your work from spilling into your personal life. Applying these strategies can improve your chances of success in your new endeavor while protecting your work-life balance.

Continuous examination of motivation

When initially exploring quiet quitting, you took time to understand and assess your "why." As you navigate your career and your personal life after quiet quitting, bringing this focus of understanding motivation to all choices—big or small—can help to keep you aligned with your long-term goals.

There are two main types of motivation: intrinsic and extrinsic. Intrinsic motivation comes from your personal beliefs, your interests, your enjoyment of an activity, or your perceptions of the world. In contrast, extrinsic motivation derives from factors outside of yourself, such as money, material rewards, or expectations of others.[48]

People motivated by personal or creative fulfillment tend to report higher job satisfaction, less burnout, and fewer difficulties completing the tasks of multiple jobs.[49] Financial or professional goals can be similarly effective motivators, but they should be specific. Pursuing new work with a specific goal in mind—such as earning enough money in your "side job" to be able to quit your full-time job within two years—is most likely to keep you motivated long-term.[50]

On the flip side, people who take on new work solely because they feel they aren't paid enough at their main job, because of obligation, or with only vague goals in mind (like making more money) tend to report low levels of job satisfaction and higher levels of burnout.[51] If your motivations align with one of these, you may want to consider choosing a more specific goal (i.e. earning money toward a vacation or mortgage payment versus simply earning more money) and/or finding a path that feels more personally fulfilling. You may even consider a different avenue entirely—such as cutting expenses instead of looking for a new job.

For any given task, in addition to considering the intrinsic and extrinsic rewards, and you can also consider:

- **Attainment value:** the benefits you get from doing a task well

- **Utility value:** the extent to which a certain task might help you achieve your goals

- **Cost:** the negative impact of completing a task.[52]

If you aren't sure what is motivating you to do a certain task, try asking yourself the following three questions:

- **Can I do this task?** This question assesses whether a task is doable autonomously. Answering "yes" suggests that you are confident in your abilities and that you believe you have power over a certain situation. The more you have power or control, the more motivated you likely are to complete a task.

- **Do I want to succeed in this task, and why?** This answer helps to determine your motivations for completing a task. Perhaps you want to succeed in writing an article for publication because you know it will help you build your writing portfolio for future jobs and because you enjoy writing—this task offers you both utility value and intrinsic satisfaction.

- **What do I have to do to succeed in this task?** This question will help you understand your volition, or the action you will take toward your goal. While your motivation usually determines whether you *want* to do something, your volition determines whether you *will* actually do it. If you have only a very vague idea of the steps necessary to do what you hope to achieve, there's less chance that you'll do it. On the other hand, if you know the specific steps you need to take, there's a higher chance you'll complete the task.

Imagine you are considering launching a side business to complement your main job. First, consider if you can do this. If you have a full day you're willing and able to dedicate to this pursuit each week and you feel prepared with the resources you need, you are likely to feel more motivated than if you have little time and the endeavor feels impossible.

Next, consider whether you want to succeed, and why. If you feel you'll get true intrinsic enjoyment from the business you're creating, you're more likely to stay motivated in the long run versus if your primary motivation is making money.

Finally, ask yourself what you need to do to start your business. The clearer the idea you have, the more likely you are to be able to move forward. You can have all the motivation in the world, but if you don't know where to start, you will likely struggle to bring the idea to fruition.

Studies of motivation show that while extrinsic factors are great motivators in the short term, they can be problematic when motivation runs out. In a study of elementary school students, researchers gave one group of children a fancy sticker for each drawing they completed. A second group received nothing. Initially, the sticker group produced far more drawings than the non-sticker group. They were even more motivated to draw in their free time. After a little while, though, some children became less motivated by the stickers and wanted bigger rewards. And when the stickers stopped, the sticker group stopped drawing almost completely while the non-sticker group continued at relatively the same rate.[53]

While you may be a little older than the subjects in this study, the same principles apply. Imagine that you create a side business making custom greeting cards in an effort to earn extra cash. If you find quick success and become overrun with more orders than expected, the relatively small prices you're charging may no longer seem like enough for the amount of effort you're putting in. And on the flip side, if your business goes through a drought with no orders, you may more easily find yourself wanting to give up entirely. In contrast, if you love creating custom cards, you'll likely feel more intrinsically motivated to get creative and find new ways to attract new customers.

So, what should you do if your main motivation to do something *is* money? Try to diversify your motivation. Even if money is the main motivator, consider what other benefits the endeavor can bring. Perhaps you realize that creating custom cards can help to enhance your portfolio. Now, whether business booms or slumps, you have a reason to stay motivated.

This examination of motivation can be applied to just about any area of your life. Whether you're considering which tasks to take on at work, how to spend your free time, or which professional growth paths to pursue, taking time to analyze these factors can help you make choices that align with your goals and keep you motivated in the long term.

Recapping chapter seven

Bringing mindfulness into every aspect of your life can help to ensure that your decision to quiet quit is worthwhile and that you fill any newly freed up time with activities that bring you benefit—unlocking the capacity to truly fully live.

- Mindfully filling any newfound free time with activities that bring you benefit will help to ensure you experience the rewards from your decision to quiet quit.

- If time with family or friends begins to feel more draining than fulfilling, try switching up your environment to remove associations and distractions.

- Consider scheduling dedicated time with friends or family—this allows you to show how much you prioritize these relationships.

- A multifaceted approach to self-care—incorporating activities to prioritize physical, social, mental, spiritual, and emotional care—can be a particularly big help in improving mental health.

- If seeking any type of new work, give yourself a specific professional or financial goal to focus on in order to stay motivated long-term. Diversifying motivations by choosing multiple goals can also be helpful.

- When deciding whether to take on a task, consider the intrinsic and extrinsic motivations, the benefits, and the costs.

While everybody's path is unique, these strategies can provide a general framework to help ensure that your decision to quiet quit is not in vain.

Conclusion

"You can't do a good job if your job is all you do."
—Katie Thurmes, co-founder of Material Change and
Artifact Uprising

A FEW YEARS AGO, I saw work-life balance as an impossible idealistic goal. Now, I've found a balance that allows me to dedicate a large part of my life to my family without a negative impact on my work. While quiet quitting brought its fair share of challenges—particularly early on—I credit it as one of the best decisions I've made in my lifetime.

Over the course of this book, we've discussed what quiet quitting really is, challenging common myths and misconceptions. Quiet quitting is a mindful approach that involves putting your needs first, and when done effectively it can benefit your employer as well.

Prior to quiet quitting, many people find themselves experiencing burnout in today's work culture. Stress can rewire your brain and cause lasting negative impact, leaving you feeling fuzzy or in a constant state of worry. Luckily, most of these effects can be undone by using neuroplasticity to our advantage and mindfully retraining our brains.

When considering quiet quitting, it is crucial to uncover your motivations. Whether you desire more time with family, space to pursue new interests, or opportunity to search for your next job, keeping your "why" top of mind will help to increase your chances of success.

Determining and setting boundaries is essential to success when quiet quitting, as it helps to ensure that you are able to hold the space you need to gain work-life balance. Continue to assess your boundaries regularly and adjust as needed to meet both work and personal needs.

Master the art of framing your boundaries in a positive light, highlighting the ways in which they help others you work with. If any conflict arises, professionally yet firmly hold your ground while listening to the other party's point of view. Look for points of similarity and focus on ways you can meet the needs of both parties without compromising your non-negotiables.

Finding ways to streamline tasks for maximum efficiency can greatly reduce your workload. Through organization, automation, delegation, and challenging perfectionist tendencies, many time-consuming tasks can become effortless. While it may take some time to structure new systems, these strategies—when implemented successfully—will save you much more time and energy in the long run.

Finally, if you choose to move forward with quiet quitting and find yourself with more free time, consider how you can best capitalize on the new opportunities in front of you. Coming back to your initial "why" can give you a starting point, but mindfully structuring your next steps will still be important to make sure you're staying aligned with your personal goals.

As you embark on the journey of quiet quitting to fully live—whether you're just starting, already on the way, or still deciding if this path is right for you—keep in mind that a small step in the right direction is the best way to begin. Start by determining and enforcing the boundaries most important to you, and build on additional boundary-setting and time-saving strategies as you're able. Take time to continuously monitor the effectiveness of any solutions you try, and don't be afraid to make adjustments as you go.

If the path ahead feels overwhelming, remember that you aren't the first person to take these steps. Many people around the world have found success in redefining their relationships with work in positive and beneficial ways. I'll leave you with a few of their words.

"I think taking vacations and turning off the phone and only doing emails or social media for a specific short amount of time helps with work-life balance. If I'm checking it all day I start to feel cuckoo-bird.... And then remembering that it doesn't matter. It just doesn't matter."

—Maria Bamford, comedian and actress

"Imagine life as a game in which you are juggling some five balls in the air.... You will soon understand that work is a rubber ball. If you drop it, it will bounce back. But the other four balls — family, health, friends, and spirit — are made of glass. If you drop one of these, they will be irrevocably scuffed, marked, nicked, damaged, or even shattered. They will never be the same."

—Brian Dyson, former vice chairman and COO of Coca-Cola

"Take care of yourself: When you don't sleep, eat crap, don't exercise, and are living off adrenaline for too long, your performance suffers. Your decisions suffer. Your company suffers. Love those close to you: Failure of your company is not failure in life. Failure in your relationship is."

—Ev Williams, co-founder of Twitter

Quiet quitting was unexpectedly and undoubtedly one of the greatest choices I ever made, and I hope that you will find similar success through applying the parts of it that best fit your situation. I wish you the best of luck on your journey toward fully living!

THANK YOU

You've made it all the way to the end!

Thank you so much for spending your valuable (and limited, considering the subject of this book!) time reading my book. I sincerely hope you've gained something worthwhile from it.

Before you go, I'd like to ask you for a favor:

Will you please consider posting a review?

I'd love to read your thoughts and see if this book has helped you as much as I hope. Your feedback is truly invaluable to independent authors like me, and could help others discover this book.

Leave a review on Amazon US:

Leave a review on Amazon UK:

ABOUT THE AUTHOR

After almost 15 years of giving 110% in an increasingly stagnant sales career, Matthew Hess realized he was leaving himself with no energy to dedicate to his passions. Most notably, Hess quickly came to resent the lack of time he was able to spend with his family following the birth of his first child. Upon discovering quiet quitting, Hess's world was flipped upside down. He learned the art of work-life balance and—surprisingly—found that the practice was mutually beneficial to both areas.

Now, Hess enjoys spending ample time outdoors with his wife Tess and children Theo and Maddie. Simultaneously, he has climbed the ranks in his corporate role and has discovered a reclaimed passion for his work. As Hess began to share his approach to quiet quitting with friends and family, he recognized that the principles could be widely applied to almost anyone. Seeing their success stories inspired him to concentrate his strategies into an accessible format to more broadly share with the world. It is his sincere hope that this book will help guide you toward your perfectly balanced life.

ALSO BY

MATTHEW HESS

Quiet Love (& Growing It)

In a world where love is often seen as a magical, predestined event or a grand gesture, many find themselves facing unrealistic expectations and shallow connections. Hess challenges these notions by introducing the concept of "quiet love"—a simple, observant, and action-based approach to nurturing relationships. Hess explains how love is not just a feeling or attraction but a series of selfless actions that improve the life of someone you care about. He debunks the myth of "love at first sight" and emphasizes the importance of growth and effort in sustaining a healthy, long-lasting relationship.

REFERENCES

1. Newport, C. (2022). The Year in Quiet Quitting. The New Yorker. https://www.newyo rker.com/culture/2022-in-review/the-year-in-quiet-quitting

2. Harter, J. (2022). Is Quiet Quitting Real? Gallup Workplace. https://www.gallup.com/ workplace/398306/quiet-quitting-real.aspx

3. Harter, J. (2022). Is Quiet Quitting Real? Gallup Workplace. https://www.gallup.com/ workplace/398306/quiet-quitting-real.aspx

4. Rosalsky, G., & Selyukh, A. (2022). The economics behind 'quiet quitting' – and what we should call it instead. NPR. https://www.npr.org/sections/money/2022/09/13/112205 9402/the-economics-behind-quiet-quitting-and-what-we-should-call-it-instead

5. Espada, M. (2022). Employees Say 'Quiet Quitting' Is Just Setting Boundaries. Companies Fear Long-Term Effects. Time. https://time.com/6208115/quiet-quitting-companies-re sponse

6. Phadke, R. (2023). Factors Affecting Job Satisfaction. Loop Health. https://www.looph ealth.com/post/factors-affecting-job-satisfaction

7. Phadke, R. (2023). Factors Affecting Job Satisfaction. Loop Health. https://www.looph ealth.com/post/factors-affecting-job-satisfaction

8. Thomas, M. (2022). What Does Work-Life Balance Even Mean? Forbes. https://www.fo rbes.com/sites/maurathomas/2022/07/26/what-does-work-life-balance-even-mean

9. Cambridge University. (2024). Meaning of work-life balance in English. Cambridge University. https://dictionary.cambridge.org/us/dictionary/english/work-life-balance

10. Thomas, M. (2022). What Does Work-Life Balance Even Mean? Forbes. https://www.fo rbes.com/sites/maurathomas/2022/07/26/what-does-work-life-balance-even-mean

11. Chiew Tong, G. (2022). Is 'quiet quitting' a good idea? Here's what workplace experts say. CNBC. https://www.cnbc.com/2022/08/30/is-quiet-quitting-a-good-idea-heres-w hat-workplace-experts-say.html

12. Chiew Tong, G. (2022). Is 'quiet quitting' a good idea? Here's what workplace experts say. CNBC. https://www.cnbc.com/2022/08/30/is-quiet-quitting-a-good-idea-heres-w hat-workplace-experts-say.html

13. Espada, M. (2022). Employees Say 'Quiet Quitting' Is Just Setting Boundaries. Companies Fear Long-Term Effects. Time. https://time.com/6208115/quiet-quitting-companies-re sponse

14. The American Institute of Stress. (2013). ComPsych StressPulse Report. https://www.stress.org/workplace-stress

15. The American Institute of Stress. (2013). ComPsych StressPulse Report. https://www.stress.org/workplace-stress

16. McEwen, B. (2017). Neurobiological and Systemic Effects of Chronic Stress. National Library of Medicine. https://www.ncbi.nlm.nih.gov/pmc/articles/PMC5573220

17. McEwen, B. (2017). Neurobiological and Systemic Effects of Chronic Stress. National Library of Medicine. https://www.ncbi.nlm.nih.gov/pmc/articles/PMC5573220

18. McEwen, B. (2017). Neurobiological and Systemic Effects of Chronic Stress. National Library of Medicine. https://www.ncbi.nlm.nih.gov/pmc/articles/PMC5573220

19. McEwen, B. (2017). Neurobiological and Systemic Effects of Chronic Stress. National Library of Medicine. https://www.ncbi.nlm.nih.gov/pmc/articles/PMC5573220

20. Pauli, W; Gentile, G; Collette, S; Tyszka, J; & O'Doherty, J. (2019). Evidence for model-based encoding of Pavlovian contingencies in the human brain. Nat Commun. Mar 07;10(1):1099.

21. Kashouty, R. (n.d.). 6 Ways Stress Affects Your Brain. Premier Neurology and Wellness Center. https://premierneurologycenter.com/blog/6-ways-stress-affects-your-brain

22. Kashouty, R. (n.d.). 6 Ways Stress Affects Your Brain. Premier Neurology and Wellness Center. https://premierneurologycenter.com/blog/6-ways-stress-affects-your-brain

23. American Psychological Association. (2018). American Psychological Association. https://dictionary.apa.org/cognitive-overload

24. McEwen, B. (2017). Neurobiological and Systemic Effects of Chronic Stress. National Library of Medicine. https://www.ncbi.nlm.nih.gov/pmc/articles/PMC5573220

25. LaVine, R. (2023). How to Manage Mental Load: 10 Strategies to Achieve Balance. Science of the People. https://www.scienceofpeople.com/mental-load

26. McGonial, K. (2015). The Upside of Stress: Why stress is good for you and how to get good at it. Avery Books.

27. England, A. (2022). People Are 'Quiet Quitting' And It Could Be Great for Mental Health. VeryWellMind. https://www.verywellmind.com/how-quiet-quitting-can-affect-our-mental-health-6502057

28. DiNardi, G. (2019). Why You Should Work Less and Spend More Time on Hobbies. Harvard Business Review. https://hbr.org/2019/02/why-you-should-work-less-and-spend-more-time-on-hobbies

29. Eschleman, K; Madsen, J; Alarcon G; & Barelka, A. (2014). Benefitting from creative activity: The positive relationships between creative activity, recovery experiences, and performance-related outcomes. Journal of Occupational and Organizational Psychology, Volume 87, Issue 3.

30. Mayo Clinic. (2023). Job burnout: How to spot it and take action. Mayo Clinic. https://www.mayoclinic.org/healthy-lifestyle/adult-health/in-depth/burnout/art-20046642

31. England, A. (2022). People Are 'Quiet Quitting' And It Could Be Great for Mental Health. VeryWellMind. https://www.verywellmind.com/how-quiet-quitting-can-affect-our-mental-health-6502057

32. Eames, H. (2024). Free vs. Paid Online Therapy in 2024: What's the Difference?. Everyday Health. https://www.everydayhealth.com/emotional-health/free-online-therapy

33. Tawwab, N. (2021). Set boundaries, find peace: a guide to reclaiming yourself. Tarcher-Perigee, an imprint of Penguin Random House LLC.

34. Glomb, M & Hulin, C. Experience sampling mood and its correlates at work. J Occup Organ Psychol. 2005;78:171–193.

35. Umiker, W. (1998). W O Management Skills for the New Health Care Supervisor. 3rd ed Gaithersburg, Md.Aspen Publishers; 1998:xxiii, 423.

36. Patterson, K; Grenny, J; McMillan, R; & Switzler, A. Crucial Confrontations: Tools for Resolving Broken Promises, Violated Expectations, and Bad Behavior New York: Mc-Graw-Hill; 2005:xviii, 284.

37. Tawwab, N. (2021). Set boundaries, find peace: a guide to reclaiming yourself. Tarcher-Perigee, an imprint of Penguin Random House LLC.

38. Patterson, K; Grenny, J; McMillan, R; & Switzler, A. Crucial Confrontations: Tools for Resolving Broken Promises, Violated Expectations, and Bad Behavior New York: Mc-Graw-Hill; 2005:xviii, 284.

39. Overton, A & Lowry, A. Conflict management: difficult conversations with difficult people. Clin Colon Rectal Surg. 2013 Dec;26(4):259-64. doi: 10.1055/s-0033-1356728. PMID: 24436688; PMCID: PMC3835442.

40. Overton, A & Lowry, A. Conflict management: difficult conversations with difficult people. Clin Colon Rectal Surg. 2013 Dec;26(4):259-64. doi: 10.1055/s-0033-1356728. PMID: 24436688; PMCID: PMC3835442.

41. Microsoft. (2023). How to use the Eisenhower matrix to prioritize your work. Microsoft. https://www.microsoft.com/en-us/microsoft-365-life-hacks/organization/how-to-use-the-eisenhower-matrix

42. Hudson, N. (2020). Are we happier with others? An investigation of the links between spending time with others and subjective well-being. Journal of Personality and Social Psychology. doi.org/10.1037/pspp0000290.

43. Hudson, N. (2020). Are we happier with others? An investigation of the links between spending time with others and subjective well-being. Journal of Personality and Social Psychology. doi.org/10.1037/pspp0000290.

44. Hudson, N. (2020). Are we happier with others? An investigation of the links between spending time with others and subjective well-being. Journal of Personality and Social Psychology. doi.org/10.1037/pspp0000290.

45. Dorociak, K; Rupert, P; Bryant, F; Zahniser, E. Development of a self-care assessment for psychologists. Journal of Counseling Psychology. 2017;64(3):325-334. doi:10.1037/cou 0000206.

46. Scott, E. (2023). 5 Self-Care Practices for Every Area of Your Life. VeryWellMind. https://www.verywellmind.com/self-care-strategies-overall-stress-reduction-3144729

47. Scott, E. (2023). 5 Self-Care Practices for Every Area of Your Life. VeryWellMind. https://www.verywellmind.com/self-care-strategies-overall-stress-reduction-3144729

48. Lai, E. (2013). Motivation: A Literature Review. Pearson.

49. Yifeng, F. (2019). Balancing the Main Act and the Side Hustle: Multiple Work Identities and Job Crafting at the Full-Time Job. Dissertation, Scheller College of Business.

50. Yifeng, F. (2019). Balancing the Main Act and the Side Hustle: Multiple Work Identities and Job Crafting at the Full-Time Job. Dissertation, Scheller College of Business.

51. Yifeng, F. (2019). Balancing the Main Act and the Side Hustle: Multiple Work Identities and Job Crafting at the Full-Time Job. Dissertation, Scheller College of Business.

52. Lai, E. (2013). Motivation: A Literature Review. Pearson.

53. Lai, E. (2013). Motivation: A Literature Review. Pearson.

Printed in Great Britain
by Amazon

56469817R10057